LIFE ON THE STREETS WITHOUT GOD AND AN EDUCATION

STEPHANIE B SCRUGGS

LIFE ON THE STREETS WITHOUT GOD AND EDUCATION

CONTENTS

DEDICATION viii
INTRODUCTION xi

CHAPTER-ONE... 1
LIFE AS A CHILD GROWING UP WITH 13 CHILDREN

CHAPTER-ONE-(CONTINUES) 9
LIFE GROWING UP AS A CHILD WITH THIRTEEN CHILDREN
BEING RAISED A SINGLE MOTHER WITH NO HIGH
SCHOOL DIPLOMA AND NO COLLEGE EDUCATION.

CHAPTER TWO 13

CHAPTER-TWO (CONTINUES) 24
BEING SAVED AT THE AGE OF NINETEEN

CHAPTER-THREE 30
LIFE IN THE MINISTRY AT THE AGE OF TWENTY-ONE

CHAPTER-FOUR.. 37
THE PRICE YOU PAY FOR NOT HAVING GOD AND EDUCATION

CHAPTER-FOUR-CONTINUES 49
THE PRICE YOU PAY FOR HAVING GOD AND EDUCATION

CHAPTER-FIVE 54
THE BENEFITS OF WISDOM THROUGH OBEDIENCE

CHAPTER-SIX.. 59
THE PRICE YOU PAY FOR BEING OBEDIENT

CHAPTER-SIX-CONTINUES............................ 61

CHAPTER-SEVEN.. 70
MARRIAGE AND BEING UNEQUALLY YOKED WITH UNBELIEVERS

CHAPTER EIGHT **75**
RAISING CHILDREN AS A SINGLE MOTHER

CHAPTER-NINE **82**
FOR I HAVE PAID MY DUES IN MY YOUTH

CHAPTER-TEN **95**
TO KNOW GOD IS TO LOVE GOD

CHAPTER-ELEVEN **106**
EVERYTHING AROUND YOU FAIL WHERE DO YOU
GO AND TO WHOM DO YOU TURN TO

CHAPTER-TWELVE **118**
WHERE THERE IS NO LOVE THERE IS NO RESPECT

CHAPTER-TWELVE-PART 2 ....**129**
BEING LIED ON, TALKED ABOUT, MISUSED, AND
ABUSE BY THE ONE YOU LOVE MOST

CHAPTER TWELVE-PART 3 .... **135**
HURTING PEOPLE HURT OTHER'S

CHAPTER-TWELVE-PART 4 .... **139**
ABUSIVE PEOPLE,ABUSIVE OTHER'S

CHAPTER THIRTEEN **141**
HE THAT WILL LIVE GODLY IN CHRIST JESUS,
MUST SUFFER PERSECUTION

**HE THAT WILL LIVE GODLY IN CHRIST JESUS
MUST SUFFER** **143**

CHAPTER-THIRTEEN-PART 2 .... **152**
THE BATTLE IS NOT GIVEN TO THE SWIFT NEITHER TO THE STRONG
BUT IT IS GIVEN TO THE ONE THAT ENDURETH TO THE END

CHAPTER-THIRTEEN-PART 3 .... **158**

CLOSING **165**
2ND CHRONICLES 20: 13-17

ALBUM **176**

DEDICATION

APOSTLE STEPHANIE B SCRUGGS

I dedicate this book to my precious **Lord and Savior Jesus Christ** Who is the head of my life, and the head of all things in my life. And, the source of everything and everybody; who will grant us all things that we desire, and the desire of our hearts. He also supplies all our needs according to his riches in glory. To the **Great** and **Almighty God** who has shown me his great love and kindness. And, the greatness of his power and his resurrection, through the miracles of signs and wonders he has performed in my life.

I also dedicate this book to my wonderful mother Mrs. Nellie Mae Scruggs who has passed on from death to life eternal. For the things she has taught me growing up as a child, with the help of our Lord who has brought me this far on this journey that has not been easy. I am now fifty-eight years old, to **GOD BE THE GLORY**

To my overseer Bishop J>R> Hopson SR., General Overseer, who has passed on from death to life. And to his most precious wife Mother Olivia Hopson, who has also passed on from death to life.

And to my home church which is in Chicago, Illinois Holiness Church of God to Pastor Elsie Brown, and the Assistant Overseer Bishop JR. Hopson Jr. Velma Larkin, Missionary Mamie Johnson, Evangelist Annie Walker, Minister Agnes Haney, wonderful Mother Davis and Deacon Davis, who is my mother and father in the Gospel, who took me under their wings, fed me and nurtured me until I could get up and walk on my own.

And most of all to Mother Vertie Austin who is my grandmother through marriage whom I appreciate very much the Word of God that was preached to me thirty-nine years ago. I'm still standing I'm still holding on, because of the word of the Lord that was preached to me on that day. I can truly say that the Word of the Lord that was preached to me fell on good ground.

IN LOVING MEMORY OF ALL MY FRIENDS IN THE GOSPEL WHOM I SHALL MEET AGAIN IN THAT GREAT RESURRECTION MORNING

Where we will never have to depart again, we will be together forever.

IN LOVING MEMORY APOSTLE STEPHANIE B. SCRUGGS

INTRODUCTION

This book consists of a family of thirteen children growing up without a dad in the home, and since I was one of the oldest, I had to help mom with the younger children while she went back to school and got her high school diploma and two college degrees. She also took on a part-time job at night to help with food for the month. As I grew into an adult, what my life was about as I turned nineteen years old. From the age of nineteen up *until the age of sixty-two. Getting* an education, getting saved at the age of fourteen. Going into the ministry at the age of twenty- one. Raising four adopted kids along my journey. Traveling over the country until the age of fifty-eight. Getting ready to build a church from the ground up, and starting a home for people with disabilities. Headed back to school to finish up my *bachelor's in accounting.*

We had a hard life growing up as a child, especially with thirteen children in the household, and the only support we had was our mother. Father ran off leaving our mother and all thirteen of the children along with her. Before departing he took a razor and cut her up nine hundred and ninety-eight stitches leaving her for dead. But she did survive that attack and started a new chapter in her life. Being the third oldest sibling had to help take care of the youngest siblings. I left home on my nineteenth birthday and moved to Chicago, Illinois to start my own life. Not knowing what lay ahead for me I just walked out by faith to start my journey. I got married at the age of nineteen and I got saved. Was put under older people who had begun to teach me the way of holiness, and how to live a Holy and sanctified life. Before God as a young adult. Started experiencing some wild things, got a job, and went back to school. Started studying for my GED and started college at the same time, to become a computer science major. Ended up getting married at the age of nineteen, which did not lead to a good ending. I started my education at Malcolm X College. The people I was around did not have any education, and they were not interested in going back to school to get any either. I found out that my husband and his people had been out there doing drugs since they were twelve and thirteen years of age. I stopped and took a good long look at them, and I told myself that this was not the life I left home to come to. I could see that they were not going anywhere in life, and I refused to let them take me down that road with them. The more I was around them, I changed courses on them. They went in one direction, and I went in another. I was not going to be persuaded by anyone to dictate my life to me and what I should have and what I should not have. I hurried up and got back to school, started working on my GED, and started taking my college courses. My husband dropped out of school in the tenth grade and never had a desire from that day to that day to go back to school and complete his education. But he chose drugs and alcohol for over forty-five years of his entire life. When the Lord began to let me see how important education is, I went for it. I visualized my life as a young adult having an education, a good job, a nice home, and a couple of fancy cars. I knew If I did not get back to school, I was going to be found in the same predicament as those that were around me.

I started the Ministry at the age of twenty-one, and I knew I needed to get back into school as soon as possible. Or else I was not going anywhere, just like the rest of those people that were around me. I took a good long look at my husband, and I could see that he did not have a care in the world. He was always trying to get out of work. He was always looking for a quick buck he did not have to work for, and that did not look good for the future. So, I started looking for a quick way to run and not look back. Then I saw the world as it was and how important it is not only to have an education but to have God in Your life as well. I am now sixty-two years of age, and as I look back, I see just. How dangerous it is not to have God and education. When you do not have a high school diploma you cannot even get a job at McDonald's now unless you have a high school diploma. And to have God in your life is even better because it goes right along with your education. I am reminded of the Apostle Paul, and he states when I was a child I spoke as a child I thought as a child, I did things as a child but when I became a man, I had to put away childish things.

CHAPTER-ONE

LIFE AS A CHILD GROWING UP WITH 13 CHILDREN

Growing up as a child, born into a family of thirteen children, wasn't too bad we had a pretty good childhood. My mother raised us by herself, and frankly, I thought that she had done a wonderful job. She provided very well for us, rent was always paid, lights were never disconnected, gas was never shut off, you can't ask for any more than that. Sometimes during the month, we got very low on food. So, we walked the neighborhood and found soda pop bottles, and cashed them in. Back in the day, the bottles were five cents, and later they rose to ten cents. We collected enough bottles to be able to buy beans, rice, chicken backs, chicken necks, or noodles. We even had enough left to buy you a snack. My mother dropped out of high school in the eleventh grade, so after having thirteen children, she decided that she needed to go back to school. By this time our father had left us and my mother had to take on the job by herself. So, she started night school and received her GED, and then she went on to the State Community College, received an Associate's Degree in auto mechanic, and then she re-enrolled into college again and received another associate's Degree in Child Care. All while she was going to school in the morning, and took a part-time job working as a cashier at a neighborhood convenience store, just to make ends meet, she was also on welfare and receiving food stamps. She survived until every one of us grew. She had always told us she wanted us to finish high school and make something out of us. She didn't want us to come down the road that she came down. She preached daily for us not to get out there and have all those children like she did. While she went to school in the morning time and worked a part-time job in the evening time, we had to try to help manage the house, until she came home at night. We came in from school in the evening and had to cook dinner for the little ones, I was the third eldest child. We had to monitor everybody's bath every night and had to see that everybody was in bed at eight-thirty. Mom came in at about nine o'clock every night. She didn't have anything to do because we knew that she needed the help so we tried to be there for her as much as possible so that the burden wouldn't be so great upon her. We struggled, but we made it. I felt so sorry for my mother growing up because of all the children she had, then had to raise us by herself. So, I helped as much as I could so that it wouldn't be so hard on her. I just kept thinking that when I get grown, I'm going to come back and help my mom with the last set of the children. I began to get older, started high school, and I became depressed, sometimes I had to walk to school and walk back home, I'm now in the eleventh grade so depressed some days I couldn't get out of bed, because of the depression. Started having a problem with my mom we started arguing, couldn't get along with her, so I dropped out of high school, and decided to enroll in Job Corp. Went off to Attu Indiana, that's when everything changed for me. I stayed there for six months and my attitude was so bad I couldn't get along with anyone. So, I got into s serious fight and they kicked me out. I met my husband in Job Corp, so when they kicked me out, I went to Chicago with my best friend, she sneaked me on the bus, and I went straight to the back and pretended like I had been on the bus all the time, so the driver walked right passed me, because I had put my coat over my head, after loading the bus the driver then took off.

I was so excited I was on my way to the windy city. The man I had met in Job Corp had already left and was already in Chicago. So, I phoned him to let him know that I was coming, and he and his father met me at the bus station. I stayed there for about thirty days, and then I got on the bus and went back to my hometown, in East St.

Louis, Ill. I didn't want to go back there because there was nothing to go back to. So, when I returned, I was confused and didn't know what I should do. So, I stayed in the house and slept most of the time. My eighteenth birthday came, and I was still in the same condition, depressed, and slept most of the time. While I was in a deep stage of depression, I was praying, because I was confused and I didn't know what to do. My heart was in Chicago, and the only thing I wanted at that time was to go to Chicago and start making a life for myself. As I was praying, I heard a voice inside tell me to pack my bags, because on my nineteenth birthday, I was leaving for Chicago. So, I washed up all my laundry and packed it into a red trunk, and I also had a brown suitcase, so every time I needed clean clothes, I would take another set of clothes out and I would wash the other set and iron them and put them back into the trunk. I continued this routine for a whole year. My nineteenth birthday is approaching.

On February twenty third nineteen seventy-eight, at one thirty-six in the afternoon, my mom took me to the Greyhound bus station, in downtown East St. Louis ILL, I had seventy-five dollars in my pocket, I bought my ticket which was about thirty-five dollars, and had fort dollars left my mom gave me thirty-five so I had seventy-five dollars in my pocket when I left home. My mom begged me not to go she thought that I was crazy being raised in a little small country town and making a huge change to move to a city that large with no relatives. She begged me not to go, but I told her that it was time now that I leave home and go out into the world and start to make a living for myself. I promised her that I would be back to help her with the last six kids who have not finished high. She begged me not to go when she saw that I was persistent, she released, me I hugged her and said my goodbyes. Six to seven hours later I was in Chicago; my friend was waiting for me at the bus station. Strange but true, both of my friends had an apartment and both said that I could live there until I got a job and could afford my own. So, I stayed with my friend that I had met in Job Corp. And they were doing drugs I didn't know that they were selling it too. I started getting depressed again, because I didn't want to end up homeless, with no place to go, no family, and people I was around didn't like me. I started putting in applications everywhere, waiting for someone to call me for a job, I didn't know what I could do, I just started riding the bus, and getting off at the first sign of factories I saw. Went home and went back out the whole week putting in applications by this time I was broke and I needed a job. Woke up one day and started crying, went into the bedroom, got on my knees, and began to pray, as I was praying I heard the telephone ring, a company by the name of Steward and Werner from the human resources department, asked me to have I found a job yet, I told her no, then she asks if I would like to come work for them, and I told her yes, she gave me my interview day and time. I went to the interview and I got the job making nine seventy-five an hour. So, when I got off the phone I started thinking, I told myself wait a minute, I was just in my room praying, for a job and the phone rang and I was hired for a job… So, I began to ponder in my heart, am there a God and if there is he just answered my prayer while I was on my knees praying. While I was praying, I was telling the Lord how sorry I was for all the bad things I had done. The bible lets us know that the goodness of God leads men to repentance. I started working the evening shift, worked for about a couple of months, and my friend was to meet me at the bus stop every night, so no one would bother me. Well one night I got off the bus, and he was not out it started to rain, and I looked down the street and saw a parked car stopped on my block in front of the apartment building where I lived. So, I focused on that car, it was doing strange things, backing up, and pulling forward, so I thought that this was strange for that car to be parked there in the middle of the street. As I approached the corner I waited on the curb for the car to pass before I crossed, and after the car had passed, I crossed the street, as soon as my foot hit the curb it started pouring down rain, and I started to run into my building and one of the guys got out of the car, with a three fifty- seven magnum and grabbed me by my wrist, put the gun to my head and he replied, I know who you are and I know what you did get into the car, I replied, and I told him he didn't know me and I haven't done anything, get your hands off me and let me go, so he started pulling me toward the car, and then I saw that he was serious. So, I began to get afraid, and I started praying again, I told the Lord if you are up there and if you are real if you get me out of this, I would do anything you want me to do. I didn't know what I was saying that was just the first thing that came into my mind. So I looked up to the sky and asked the Lord again to help me while the man was still pulling me to the car, I started resisting, and I heard the voice of God, tell me to fall on my knees and do exactly like he told me to do, so I started trying to reason with the voice I heard, and the Lord spoke to me again and said don't argue with me, I immediately fell on my knees and I had a butcher knife in my purse, I was going to stab him before I got into the car, but I heard the voice of the Lord say do not pull that butcher knife out, I fell on my knees and I heard the voice of Lord say, come up on your hands, and when you get up to take off and run, and I'm going to bless you, and so it was I got up and I took off and they took my purse with the butcher knife and my Identification card. When I got to my front door my friend was coming out of the basement apartment with his father. I started crying and telling him what had happened, and we called the police, but I couldn't identify them because it was dark.

About a month later I heard the voice of the Lord again, he spoke to me and said, you told me that if I get you out of that situation, you would do anything, and then I replied yes Lord. He then told me to find me a church to go to, and if I find a church and start going, he was going to bless me and no one else will ever touch me again... I was very frightened now, so I started taking studies with the Jehovah's Witnesses. I took about three studies with them, and I went out of the house one day and walked around the corner to the store, and I saw a church, on the corner, it was a Baptist church, I heard the voice of the Lord speak to me and said, that's not it. Jehovah's Witnesses came to the house again and gave me a bible, I started reading it, and I understood everything I had read. So, Jehovah's Witnesses started teaching me that living with a man and not married to him is a sin. So, I told myself well they don't know that I'm living with this man. And I couldn't sleep behind that it started worrying me, and I felt convicted, and I couldn't sleep. So, when Jehovah's Witnesses came again, they said it again.

I started reading my bible and I called up my boyfriend's sister to ask her, she didn't know, so she called up her grandmother, and she gave me her grandmother's phone number, I called her up and asked her, and she gave me her answer, then she asks me what church do I go to, I replied to her that I didn't have a church home and that I was taking study's with the Jehovah Witnesses, then she replied that I need to get out of that, because they weren't right. She then asked me to come and go to church with her, I told her that I would, but the next Sunday I went back to the Kingdom Hall, and then I got confused because now I don't know who is right and who is wrong. So, I went back into my room and began to pray and ask the Lord what should I do which direction should I go, and who was right and who was wrong. So, I got up and got my bible and I had the King James version and when I opened the bible up, it opened to the book of Jeremiah, and it stated that they ran but I didn't send them, then the Lord spoke to me and said don't go back to the Kingdom Hall, he then told me on a Saturday evening to call up my boyfriend's grandmother and go to church with her so I did.

I started praying again, and then I asked the Lord about living with that man and not married to him was it a sin, I then got my bible again and opened it up to the book of Mathew, and the Lord was speaking to me through his word, and then he told me that it was a sin so that started worrying me, I knew that I had to get myself out of that situation. I called Mother Austin up and I told her that I wanted to go to church with her, so she told me to meet her on the corner of Ogden and Pulaski, so non- Sunday morning we met at that location, but the church was not open, and she didn't know why, so we got on the bus, and went upon Roosevelt Rd, to Pastor Oder Wright church. Service had started the people were shouting speaking in tongues, and praising the name of the Lord. It was so beautiful, to see the people speaking in another language, so while I was sitting there, I told the Lord that I wanted to do that too. The pastor started preaching, and it was so marvelous the way he was preaching, he then preached from the book of Isaiah, stating how Mary was going to bring forth a son, and shall call his name Emmanuel, and how he was going to save his people from their sins. I told God sitting there that I never knew that Jesus came and died for me so that I might be saved. So, after the preaching an alter call was made, and the pastor asked if anybody would like to give their life to the Lord after hearing the message, so Mother Austin pushed me and said go ahead so I got up to go to be baptized and the missionaries came and got me and took me back to get ready for my baptism. So, it's my time to go down in the water, they had me to repeat after them, and ask the Lord to forgive me of all my sins, so I did.

After church, we had to go home, and come back, because they were starting a revival. As I went outside, something strange had taken place. The trees were so round and pretty green that they looked like trees in heaven. The grass had gotten greener and the sky was so pretty and blue, and the clouds looked like something I had never seen before, the clouds looked like they had so much power in them. I still didn't understand what had happened to me, so I went home and told my boyfriend about it, then he followed me back to the church that same night, he then repented and got baptized that same night. We continued to go to the revival for that week. Then we had to start working on the situation about shacking so we decided that we were going to get married, and Mother Austin told me to wait a while, so I didn't listen, then the pastor married us so I didn't have that conviction hanging over my head for shacking.

A few weeks went past and I came out of the house one night and went around the corner to the store, when I came out I crossed the street, and I saw a man crossed behind me so I heard the voice of the Lord say stand by the fence and hold on to it because that man was going to try to rob me, so he walked up on me and said keep walking, and he had a gun, he then replied do you have any money so I had a small coin purse and my bible was in it, then replied that I didn't have any money and that the only thing I had was my bible. So, then he took off and left me alone. The Lord had performed his word when he spoke to me and said if I would go to church, he would shield me and protect me so that nobody would ever bother me again.

LIFE GROWING UP AS A CHILD WITH THIRTEEN CHILDREN BEING RAISED A SINGLE MOTHER WITH NO HIGH SCHOOL DIPLOMA AND NO COLLEGE EDUCATION.

As you know, I can testify for myself, that there is a reality in serving a true and living God. You must have that experience to be able to testify to this. As I started at the age of nineteen, I started with nothing and I had to grow into something. I chose to grow into that which was right and righteous. The path you choose that's what you must live with for the rest of your days. I stepped out on faith when I left East, St. Louis Illinois at the age of nineteen. It was kind of scary, although a very dear friend of mine had a place set up for me to come, that was a blessing in itself. Got my GED accumulated credit hours in Computer science and completed one year of learning how to operate all the input-output devices, and learn how to operate all the hardware and software. And graduated. Started driving commercial vehicles, and in 2000 started a truck driving school and completed that possessing a class A with all the endorsements. In 2001 went back to Sinclair College and got my Real- Estate Degree. And got my appraisal certificate. Now I have e few things I can do along the way. Adopted four children, and now they have their own children. One is a nurse, one is an engineer, and one got a four-year free ride to the University of Indianapolis, and majored in accounting, and now he is the auditor for the city of Indianapolis. I also have close to sixty hours in computer science, which I'm getting ready to use to go back to school to major in accounting. I'm getting ready to retire from driving the buses and trucks and getting ready to purchase land so that I can put down single-family module homes for people with disabilities. And I'm getting ready to build a ministry from the ground up, I have been in the evangelist field for thirty-seven years. Had a job in every city I went in. Learning how to operate motor coaches and transit buses, I could find a job very quickly in every city I went in. I also started school again in Dayton, Ohio for Business Administration. So, now I can take those credit hours into accounting and get my accounting degree so that I can be able to manage my finances and payroll. It's going on forty years now, God has never left me or forsaken me. He has told us in his word that he would be with us through thick and thin. He let us know that he would never leave us or forsake us, and I can truly testify to his words. He's a God that cannot lie neither is he the son of man that he should repent, if he said it, he shall perform just what his word has said. I only had two more semesters to have my associate's degree in computer science. Things in the marriage got so bad that I got depressed because my husband stopped bringing his paycheck home to pay the bills. I dropped out and went to a trade school for computer operations for a year and I did graduate. I had to find a job in the meantime while I finished this year. For all the good jobs I had, I had to have a high school diploma. Most of my jobs were driving for the transit authorities in the different states I went in to preach. I don't think that I would have gone this far in life without God. I would have never accumulated what I have. accumulated if it had not been for me to go back to school and get an education which led to being able to get these good jobs from the state, driving commercial vehicles. In life having God and education along with it brings forth happiness and joy. When I'm able to pay my bills I'm at peace with myself, therefore it is so important to go to school so that you don't have to depend upon government assistance. They dictate how much you should have once a month, anybody in their right mind would not wait on a check one time out of the month, and food stamps for you and your children once a month. I grew up on a once-a-month check and food stamps once a month. My mother was receiving food stamps once a month and government assistance once a month. We always ran out of food the last week of the month, and my mom had to sell some of the food stamps to be able to pay all the bills for the whole month. I saw her struggle; I always had a sad spirit for my mom. I told her when I was grown, I would be back to help her and help her with the other children that she had left to grow. Even when we ran out of food the last week of the month, we went and walked the neighborhood to find pop bottles. Back in the sixties and the seventies, pop bottles were five cents, and then they increased to ten cents a bottle. We had found enough to get at least five to six dollars off the pop bottles. And then sometimes we would trade them in go back and get them and trade them in for the second time. And then the people at the store got wise and they started marking the bottles across with a black magic marker. So, we took some alcohol wiped the bottles off, and traded the same bottles back in again. We could buy beans and rice chicken backs and chicken necks and corn meal to make bread to go with the beans and rice. We also had money left to buy a bag of popcorn for all of us before bedtime. My mom went back to school as soon as she had the thirteen kids, and she also got a part-time job around the corner, at the neighborhood store. As I grew up, I realized how important it was for us to go to school and get an education, because our childhood was the best as anyone can expect it to be. We did not want to grow up like our mom with all those children and end up on welfare. Out of thirteen children, only two did not complete high school and did not go. to college. One boy and one girl. My mom struggled to get us through high school and struggled to see to us finishing. I desired to never go through what my mom had to go through; it was very tough. When my mom went back to school, she got her GED and then she went on to state community college and got an Associate's degree in auto mechanics then when she graduated, she went back again and got another associate's degree in teaching. So, now she has two degrees. She used her auto mechanic degree to fix her cars, she even taught the boys how to fix cars. Then she worked as a teacher until she died in 2005. She could go to work and support the last eight children on an earned income, instead of continuing welfare. She had told us many times not to have all those children, and go to school and get an education so that we would not have to depend upon the welfare system. Out of thirteen children, only one ended up on welfare and refused to go and get an education until President Bill Clinton put an end to being on welfare your entire life. So, she had no other choice but to find a job go to work, and stop depending upon the federal government to take care of you and your children. I have also completed thirty- seven years in the ministry, and almost forty years being saved, walking with God for almost forty years has been a great experience. It has been an experience of a lifetime; I wouldn't take anything for the journey that I have had with the Lord. The life I have had is getting better and better. Life brings about a change.

CHAPTER TWO

___

People love you from their mouths, but their hearts are far from it. Anybody can say that they love you but turn around the next second and talk about you like you were nothing. They will gossip and lie to you and turn right back around and tell you that they love you. For you to walk around with a double tongue and a forward mouth, you have no love neither do you have any respect. Where there is no love, there is no respect. Because love will not allow you to lie to your brother or sister. Neither will it allow you to harm a person you are supposed to have love and respect for. Even in our own families, there is no love nor is there any respect. And these things ought not to be said the Lord. Then I also had to deal with the disrespect of the church, and this ought not to be. If you are to represent The Love of God, you must show it every day of your life, not only on Sundays but every day of the week. Not only to the household of faith but also to your blood family. You do not go around in the world and treat strangers better than you treat your own family; this should not be so. We have got the word of God mixed up. How can we profess that we love God and hate our sister and brother, the word of God says we are a liar, and the truth is not in us. Your works speak for you, so therefore do not allow your mouth to say one thing, and your actions are doing something different. Allow your thoughts and your actions to work together, so that you will not be held in contempt when the Lord Jesus shall appear, and we must stand before the Great White Throne to give an account of every deed that was done in this body. Learn how to be righteous in everything that you do. Jesus had given the disciples a command: And that commandment was for them to love ye one another, as I have Loved you. When you possess the Love of God you will not intentionally hurt people because of your Ill intentions, and the jealousy that rules you from the inside. Jealousy, hatred, envy, and strife cause you to harm people for no good reason. We find many family members fighting all the time, maybe one has a little bit more than the other, and if that's the case why not try to help the one that doesn't have it don't have to be money at all the time, maybe they need personal things now and then. And most of the time they do not know what they are fighting about. And the disrespect goes on for years. We must remember that when things like that take place in a family, that is a generational curse. And somebody must be strong enough and have enough Love for God in them to stand against, the wicked devices of the devil. Jealousy, hatred envy, and strife, talking against your sister and your brother for no good reason is of the devil. We did not hear about Jesus talking against the disciples one to another. So why are we going around spreading people's business across the country, most of the time it's just gossip and lies because where there is no love there is no respect. Love and respect will cause you to do the right thing by all men because Love and respect are of God. After family members have been disrespectful to one another for years and years, then when one has passed away, and you didn't make amends with them, then it's on your conscious for the rest of your life. This is why you have to treat everybody with Love and respect, so that when something does happen you can say they you have done your best, and you don't have to worry about not being able to sleep at night because of the disrespect that you have shown them down through the years. Where there is no Love there is no respect, how can you have Love for someone and don't have respect for them? How can you say that you love God and hate your sister and your brother, for you are a liar, and the truth is not in you, because you see them every day, and you do not have any love for them nor do you have any respect for them? But God is a Spirit, we pray to someone that we don't see, but we say that we Love God, and people the things ought not to be. Love ye one another as Christ has Loved us. For we know that we are in the last days, and because we are in the last days, the love of many has waxed cold.

More and more each day, we see mother against daughter, daughter against mother, father against son, son against father, sister against sister, brother against brother. Where there is no love there is no respect.

I raised four adopted children from small children, and as they started growing into adolescence, their attitude and their personality started coming out, we must realize that what is on the inside of you is going to start to show on the outside of you. The disrespect started coming out, so therefore by you showing me how disrespectful you are, I knew then that they did not have any love for me. Because if they did, Love doesn't have you being disrespectful to the person who has adopted you and caring for you, where there is no love there is no respect. They started openly rebellion and dared to me say anything to them. Well, I'm the type of person I'm not going to allow you to run over me in my house. They started doing things to deliberately aggravate me, they knew the things that would make me mad. Just like my oldest nephew, every time I leave home, I would give them chores to do, after I'm gone, he tells them that they don't have to do anything I said because I was nobody's mother, where there is no love, there is no respect. I took those children to church every Sunday, and I cannot understand for the life of me how they turned out the way that they did. I was sad for many days, about their life. But there was nothing that I could do. I heard the voice of the Lord say that all the children were leaving, he told me that he was going to scatter them all over the country, and he said when he was done punishing them for their behavior, and for the disrespect that they had committed against me in my own home that they will be back to ask for forgiveness. I put the oldest nephew out for staying out in the streets all night long thinking that he could walk in my house anytime he wanted to and started drinking and using drugs. I was not getting ready to tolerate that out of nobody's children, so I showed him the door, I sent him to East St. Louis, Illinois to my mother's house, and from there he went to the military, and got beat up, and kicked out because of no respect for his Superior Officers.

Where there is no love there is no respect. His life started going downhill from there. After taking them to church every Sunday people would give me high praises on how well-mannered these children were, but they did not know the hidden secret about them outside of church, and inside of my home. But God knew and he was not going to allow me to be deceived in my own home. They would get up and testify and thank the Lord for giving them a family that cared about them and loved them, that was all a lie, where there is no love there is no respect. It wounded me so badly to take someone else's child in my house, and because of one bad apple that was in the basket, it caused the whole basket of apples to get rotten. My God help us today, to walk circumspectly, not as fools, but as wise. For we will in this life reap everything we have sown, whether it has been good, or whether it has been evil. So, the Lord put an end to it all they all walked out and left, my thought was if you can do a better job for yourself at the age of thirteen and fifteen, I recommend that you keep moving and try to do the best you can for yourself. I was only trying to teach them how to survive, anytime your biological parents allow you to go to foster care and do not even try to come back and get you, nor even try to contact you, why would you get adopted and show nothing but disrespect in the adopted mothers home, when your biological parents gave you up and walked away. Where there is no love there is no respect, you must learn to have respect for the one that is taking care of you, because the one that is taking care of have to have some type of love for you for them to adopt you and allow you to live in their home until you were grown. Clothes, shoes, food, and raiment were provided for you, and when you look back there was nothing that you needed, everything was provided for you including a nice clean home where there was not much for you to do except to keep your living quarters clean, and you didn't even want to do that. School fees were paid every semester, new uniforms were bought every school year, lunches were provided, and you got an allowance, I allowed you to earn extra money, what more could I have done, I was not appreciated for all that I did for everybody, because where there is no love there is no respect. I'm sorry you walked out and had to go through what you are going through, but I couldn't allow you to run over me in my house. We all make mistakes, but after we realize that we have made a huge mistake, we need to learn how to ask God to forgive us and ask that person we have so wronged for forgiveness so that we can have a piece of mind behind the behavior you exercised. Sometimes when we are young the devil makes us think that the grass is greener on the other side of the fence, when you cross over that fence and get to the other side, you find that the grass has not been watered, and the temperature of the sun has scorched the grass until it has died. And now the guilt sets in, you see that the grass was not so green on the other side of the fence. But you still don't dare to humble yourself and ask for forgiveness. Where there is no love, there is no respect. I was even threatened by one of them with the cops, so I had to paddle her for her behavior, I was only trying to bring her up in a way, so she could be wise and not let men trick her, and get all those kids, and end up taking care of them on her own. So, they thought my teaching was wrong I had to allow them to go where they were going and do a better job for themselves than I was doing. What do you know at the age of thirteen, nothing, where there is no love there is no respect? So, after I had been threatened by the police, I told her she had one more time to open her mouth to me in my home, she waited for about three months, and she did it again, I patted her again, and then she had the nerve to talk crazy to me in front of company. I patted her right in front of the company, and I told her if the company didn't like it, they could get some too. After the company left, I went upstairs and dealt with her again, because I saw that she had gotten out of hand, so I told them to get their clothes ready for tomorrow, and on Monday I called children's services. I had warned her that when she came home on Monday children's services were going to be waiting on her. Well, someone set the clock early that morning, so I got up and went downstairs on the couch, and waited for them to get dressed and have their breakfast, I wanted to make sure she didn't sneak any clothes out of the house. My motto was you came with nothing and you will leave with nothing period. So, after they left for school, I called children's services to report her behavior and to let them know that she could not continually live in my house talking to me crazy like she was the momma and I was her child that will never happen in my world. So, when I called them, they told me Ms. Scruggs if she doesn't show back up at home, this is what I want you to do, call the police and put a warrant on her, then take her down to the courthouse before the judge, then I replied ok I surely would. I decided not to go to school, that particular day, and I lay waiting on the coach, about three-fifteen of the other two kids came home, but she did not. So, I called the police to come to the house, and I made a run-away report on her. And later that night she still didn't show up. I felt her presence around the apartment complex, then I knew that she was in the area. So, the next day I asked the other two kids to go to the office and call me if she shows back up at school. So, I was lying across my bed and I was in a deep dream, and she was in the dream, and I saw her standing, and she had on her faded jeans, white T-shirt, and white sneakers. So, the phone rang and it was her sister, so all three of the children were in the same grade, and they had a class together, so she called me to let me know that Jasmine showed up at school. I told her thanks for calling I'm on my way. I got dressed and called the police on my way out the door. So, Huber Heights police met me at the school, and they went into her classroom and escorted her out, I asked them If they could escort her down there because if she opened her mouth to me again while she was in my car, I'm going to pull the car over and get her again. So, they explained to me that they were not allowed to transfer children down to the courthouse anymore so, I asked the officer if he could talk to her about not opening her mouth, so the officer took her to the back room, and told her something, but I didn't hear what the officer had told her, because when she came out of the room she was screaming and crying. Where there is no love, there is no respect, when someone opens their mouth up to you and speaks whatever comes to their mind, and doesn't care how they say it, a child is supposed to be taught, and no child is supposed to be teaching the parents. I headed down to the courthouse took her in and registered her, we then had to go into the intake room to give our statement. After giving our statement, they called in Children's Services to come, and then Children Services called up an emergency foster parent. The foster parent arrives and she falls out in the middle of the floor and begins screaming, I told her that you should have thought about that before you started opening your mouth to me, and you thought that you were going to get away with it. I warned them so many times that this was going to happen if they tried running over me in my house. I walked out of the courthouse and left her right there. Unit three days later, we had to go before the Judge. I showed up at court three days later she was there with her new foster parent, and children services. We were asked to go into the courtroom, and her attorney was also present because the judge told Children Services to get her a lawyer. So, we went back to court, and Children Services tried to get the judge to release the case from his courtroom and send it over to the guardianship court, the Judge asked me If I wanted to send the case to the other court or try the case in his courtroom, I replied, judge due to all respect, I would like to keep the case here in your court. So, he found her to be unruly and ungovernable. He put her on probation until she was eighteen. And told her that he did not want to see her again in his courtroom. He told her how he was in his chambers watching her disrespect me in the courthouse and how she should have been thankful that somebody of my character had adopted her and her brother together. The judge told her that it is so many children that would love to have a mother like Ms. Scruggs. So many children out there who would never have a chance to get adopted, and you got an adoption placement and did not appreciate it. So, the Judge asked Children's Services what they were all going to do with her, and they replied that they were going to do an investigation on Ms. Scruggs and send her back. Where there is no love there is no respect. Because love doesn't have you disrespecting your elders. The Judge told Children's Services; no, you are not going to put her back in Ms. Scruggs's home because Ms. Scruggs said that she can't come back to her home. He asked children's services where she came from, they replied Hamilton County, I replied no she did not come from Columbus, Ohio. The judge told them to go back and pull her file, find a long-lost uncle, and send her back to them. And the judge said maybe on down the road Ms. Scruggs can forgive her and they can make amends and get back together. I decided to move out of Dayton, Ohio, and move to Indianapolis. After I got into Indianapolis the brother and my niece decided to do the same thing that their sister did. I came home from work early one night and found my niece and her brother in my bedroom watching pornography on my computer. So, I had to whip their butts. And they had allowed all the children into my apartment, to eat up all the snacks and soda pops, and then trashed the house. So, I made them clean it up, and the next night I came home early the next day, because I had gotten into an argument with someone on the job, and then walked out and quit. I came home again and as I was driving up the street, I saw a light on the building across from my building, I looked up at my bedroom window, and the light was coming from my bedroom, as I parked the car, I was on the phone talking to my mother, and I told her that they were in my bedroom again, she said that I was lying, I told her to stay on the phone I was going to sneak up there and catch again in my bedroom. I sneaked upstairs and walked into my bedroom, the boy was sitting in my computer chair, my computer watching pornography. I stood in the back of him for a good minute, and he finally looked around and saw that it was me and humped up and started screaming. I grabbed him and whipped his but, but the girl had been watching out for me she had already seen me out there and didn't warn him, she allowed him to take the wrap by himself. So, when I went to go to her room, she already had the door locked, with a chair behind it, I didn't even ask her to open the door, I proceeded and kicked it in and I paddled her about along with him. So, I drove to St. Louis to pick up my mother to come back and watch the house, when I and my mother returned from St. Louis, she made the kids clean the house back up and made them eat peanut butter and jelly sandwiches. Where there is no love, there is no respect. So, on Monday morning both of the children went to school and one came home and the other didn't get off the bus. He had ditched school and started running around with all those bad kids, setting around the apartment complex and setting off fire alarms in all the buildings. The sheriff kicked him up during the course of the night, and they came to my door with him in the back of the squad car and gave me a number to call and told me where he was taking him, and for me to call that number the next day. So, the next day I waited outside in the car and my mother, and when my niece came in from school, I told her to give me my keys and get into the van, then we went to the place where Roy was and I gave my statement, colleen went into a room and I never seen neither one of them again. Colleen and Roy said that they didn't want to go back and live with that woman. Where there is no love, there is no respect, because respect will not allow you to have sex in your mother's bed. And love will not have you been evil towards someone who took time out of their busy schedule to adopt you and give you a permanent place to live, and that is the gratitude that you have toward them calling them in the courtroom that woman. Where there is no love there is no respect. So, both of them were put into a residential center for three months, and then we went to court, and they told so many lies against me that I didn't have the strength nor the energy left to keep fighting against the evil that was present in my home. When Roy got on the stand, he addressed me as that woman, I looked at him and the Judge stepped in and said you listen up young man, don't you ever come into my courtroom and address someone as being that woman, he said if you don't want to call her your mother to address her as Ms. Scruggs. So, after the trial, the judge ordered children's services to find a foster home to put them in. And then the Judge asked me if I wanted visitations, I said no because I didn't put them there. So, Colleen said that she didn't want to go with grandma.

I told my mother to come on I left the courtroom, and I told my mother to take your time and walk, so, I ran out of the court house went and got my car, drove up to the door, and picked up my mother, and we left. I spent over twenty years raising adopted children which was so ungrateful and disrespectful. I find so many people in life that have gotten caught up in the system and people just had to let them go, because when you get to a point in life where nobody can't tell you anything, then you are going to have to learn the hard way. That means everything you do is going to be complicated for you because you have refused to receive instructions. I didn't get this far in life not accepting instructions. So, I have not seen them since, until this day. I had given up my dreams so that they may have a chance for education. I found out one thing in life you can't make a person take or accept the things that you want for them. I provided everything for them and it still wasn't enough for them. They walked away and in other words, they were telling me to kiss their butt, and that they didn't need me, so, sad I was so hurt it took me a long time to get over that, and I am still not quiet over the matter yet. For where there is no love there is no respect. I did love the children, but I could not understand what I had done wrong to them for them to be allowed in my house and turn around and disrespect me the way they did. But going through the storm it made me stronger. It also opened up my eyes to people in general, I feel like people you live with every day can wake up in the morning and pretend like they love you. What would you think about people you meet outside of your circle? I have managed to keep my eyes and ears open toward people in general. Jesus said that in the last days, because inequity has abounded, the love of many has waxed cold. Nobody in this day and hour, has any respect for anybody. Nevertheless, life goes on, and therefore I started a new chapter in my life. So, know a new chapter begins.

Behold, the hour cometh,yea, is now come,
That you shall be scattered

Every man to his own, and shall
Leave me alone, and yet I am not alone,
Because the Father is with me
JOHN 16:32KJV

These things I have spoken unto you,
That in me you might have peace.
In the world ye shall have tribulation:
But be of good cheer; I havae overcome the world.
JOHN 16:33KJV

CHAPTER-TWO
(CONTINUES)

BEING SAVED AT THE AGE
OF NINETEEN

The journey began for me at the age of nineteen, was nineteen years old when I left East St. Louis Ill, and moved to Chicago. Ill., I Thought that I was getting ready to move to a big city and have some fun, but the Lord had other plans for me when

I got there were there for less than six months when a tragedy almost happened to me, I almost got snatched off the street, that made me so afraid, so I started going to church. And accepted the Lord as my savior. When the man snatched me on the west side of Chicago, and he had a three fifty-seven magnum in his hand and tried to drag me to the car, I began to pray, I asked the Lord if he was real, up there please save me and get me out of this I looked up to heaven and began to pray, I heard a voice from heaven, and it told me to fall on my knees, I looked up again and I said I can't be falling on my knee's I need to try to get away. I put my hands in my purse to get the butcher knife out, and I heard the voice saying don't pull the butcher knife out. So, I left the butcher knife in the bag and fell on my knees, and the voice spoke again and said don't argue with my fall, I fell on my knees and the voice told me when I come up real slow on my hands and he was going to bless me two getaway and so I did, I got up and took off and ran and got through the door. In the meantime, I got saved, went back to school, got my GED, and started college, majoring in Computer programming. I got saved because the people I had got hooked up with were on drugs. And I was frightened that someone grabbing me again. About two weeks later

I heard a voice again and he told me that I said if he blessed me to get away, I would do anything. So, I answered and said yes, and the voice told me to start looking for a church to go to. And the voice said If I start going to church, they would shield me and protect me, so nobody would ever touch me again. So, I started walking around the neighborhood looking for a church, I saw a Baptist church I heard the voice of the Lord saying that's not the one. I saw another Baptist church in the neighborhood, and he said that's not the one either. So, Jehovah's Witness came to the door and I started taking studies with them for about three weeks. They started off teaching about living with a man and was not married to him as a sin. They came back the next week and said the same thing. So, I started pondering in my heart I needed to get myself out of this. So, I wanted to know something in the bible so I called up my boyfriend's sister. So, she didn't know, and she said we could call her grandmother, she would know because she was an ordained minister. So, we called her up, and she asked me what church was I going to I told her to the kingdom hall. So, she told me to get out of that and come and go to church with her. The next Sunday I got kind of confused, so I went back to the kingdom hall the next Sunday. The next week I stopped taking the studies with them and on that next Sunday, I called her up on that Saturday and she told me where to meet her, and we met up on that Sunday. The church we were supposed to be going to was closed. So, we went up on Roosevelt Road and found a church. So, I went in that morning and got saved and baptized the same day. I felt like I had to do this for me because I saw a road I didn't want to go down. The people I was around didn't want anything, nor did they want to do anything for themselves. They didn't finish high school, and neither were they considering going back to try to accomplish some type of gold in life. A year had gone by and the people around me still didn't even try to do anything for themselves, instead they were stealing and robbing just to get drugs and alcohol. I messed around and married the man I met in Job Corps. His grandmother was the one that took me to church and I got saved. My husband was caught up with them. He went back to the church that same night and repented and got baptized, but he messed around and started playing games with the lord. He started stealing and robbed my house, so I had to move away from them. A year into the marriage, things begin to go downhill very fast. My husband stopped bringing his paycheck home, and one Friday I asked him why didn't come home and give me some bus fare to go to church, he replied this is my money and you don't tell me what I should and shouldn't do with my paycheck. So, I was in college at that time and I switched over and went to a computer learning school where I learned how to operate all the I/O equipment. So, I graduated from the Computer Learning Center and found a job. I started making at least three to four dollars more than he was making. So, I vowed a vow that I would never if I lived depend upon another man again to take care of me, I kept a job, and paid my way through life with the help of the Lord. My husband became more and more addicted to those drugs he decided that he didn't want to be saved, and now I'm stuck with a drug addict. I didn't realize that the worst was yet to come, sorrows for me being saved as a young adult have just begun. He started messing up all the money, wouldn't pay any bills, lied stole the rent money, and did everything he could to hurt me. I stayed in the church the saints told me to hold on, and keep praying because the husband is sanctified through the sanctified wife. I went to church three to four times a week, and every time I went to church, I was always crying. Went to work and finished school, but things have not gotten easy, it was getting worse and worse. So, two years have gone past, one night I was reading my bible before I went to bed and the voice of the Lord spoke to me and said don't go to school today, he wanted me to stay home and fast, so I did just that. As I got up that morning the Lord spoke to me and said get your bible, I got my bible and when I flipped it open it opened to the book of Isaiah and the spirit of the Lord started Ministering to me, and he began to speak to me and say that he was anointing me to preach the Gospel. After he had finished, I got up and said, the Lord is calling me to the Ministry. It was very hard being saved at a young age back in that day and time, but glory is to God, I had quite a few mentors who counseled me during that time. When I didn't go to school. I went over to Mother Austin's house, Mother Davis, and Deacon Davis's house we would have prayer, then we started bible study and Mother Davis would fry chicken and make vegetable soup, and she would always make me some tea cakes. Then I had Evangelist Walker and Minister Haney, they were always there for me. I could call them anytime, and they were always there for me to pray for me. The first six to seven years were very hard for me because I didn't understand many things, I thought that everything was going to be very easy since I had given my life over to the Lord. I started complaining a lot, my marriage got worse and worse, I just didn't want to be in the marriage anymore. I tried to get rid of him but he refused to go. The drug dealers were at my home one day I came in and he approached me about my husband owing him money for drugs he got on credit, so they wanted to try to hurt me along with him I told him, that I don't do drugs, the only thing I do is preach the Gospel, I began to minister to him, I told him that whatever business you have with him take it outside and please don't come back in my house with that foolishness. So, they took it outside and he ended up giving up his wedding band for the drugs. Life had become very difficult even since I accepted my calling in the ministry. The more I prayed the worse things became. I started going down to the church for shut-in fasting and praying for three days and three nights with no food and water, I didn't understand why, but down the road, I was going to need that power for what I had to go through. My husband ended up overdosing three or four times, he tried to kill himself a couple of times, and ended up in the mental hospital numerous times, I still didn't understand what I was dealing with, and now we have started praying, and they began to teach me how to deal with spirits in the other world, it was very scary at first, but I had to stay in the word and not be afraid. The things that he had put himself through I wouldn't wish that life on my worst enemy. The more I saw where his life was going, I made up my mind that I was going to stay with the Lord, I didn't want to go down that path. The drugs and alcohol had taken over him and his family. I couldn't sleep at night I became very fatigued and nervous, always worrying I tried to be there for him, but he would not accept my help. I still didn't understand what the problem, was and why those things were happening. We took him back to church and tried to help him get saved but he wanted to play games and pretend as if he had gotten saved, but it didn't work he went right back out there and continued to use drugs, we worked and worked with him but nothing happened, now I was ready to dump him and get a divorce. I could see down the road, and I knew that he didn't want to be saved, and I knew that he would never give over to the Lord because he didn't want God and God will not force himself on anybody. His life was all the reason I needed to stay with the Lord at all costs. I looked at his life and I took a good look at mine, everything seemed to be working for me. My pathway was smooth, and everything I asked the Lord for granted to me. All that fasting and praying I had done the Lord knew that down the road I would need it because the Lord knew what was going to befall me down that road because of the type of person I got mixed up with. I didn't let his lifestyle interfere with the life I had with God. I was persuaded within my mind that the devil was out to turn me back on him to start using drugs and alcohol with him. His life lesson was a good enough reason for me not to go that path. My mother was so surprised when I told her I got my GED started College, and got a good job. Therefore, it is important to be able to think for yourself so that you would not be misled by anyone. He thought that since I came from a little small town, he could use me, he wanted to help pay for me to go to school so that I could take care of him. Well, he got fooled. But because I gave my life over to the Lord when I was Nineteen years God blessed me, and not only did he bless me but God kept me so that I wouldn't let go. I encourage you to get God to hold on to him because Jesus is coming back again, to rapture the church. And I want to be able to go back with the Lord when he comes and crack the sky, and the trumpet shall sound and the Lord is going to say come to my people. I hope you get hold of God and don't let him go for anybody. Hold on Hold on.

Trust Ye In the Lord Jehovah Forever:
For in The Lord Jehovah Is Everlasting Strength
Isaiah; 26:2

CHAPTER-THREE

LIFE IN THE MINISTRY AT THE AGE OF TWENTY-ONE

I've been saved now for two years, was enrolled in college, major was computer science. I was called to the ministry at the age of twenty-one. Trials and tribulations are becoming harder and harder. My trials were in my home and the church. My husband had become addicted to drugs. He started messing up the paycheck. I only had two more semesters to go to have my degree in computer science. I was doing good I was getting A's and Bs in college. I became two depressed because he didn't want to bring the money home to pay the bills until I finished the last two semesters. I enrolled in the Computer Learning Center, to learn how to operate all the input- output devices and I found a job to help support myself so I wouldn't have to depend upon anybody for anything but God. Well, we started splitting the bills I paid half on everything. I got paid every Wednesday, and he got paid on Fridays. Every Wednesday I had him come up to the job and get the fifty dollars for the car payment, come to find out he and his friend took the money and smoked it up. I asked him to not bring his friend to my house. Every time I left and went to work, he and his friend would use the house to do drugs. Well, his friend brainwashed him against me, just to get his paycheck to smoke the whole checkup every week. The car place went into his job and started garnishing his paycheck because he chose to smoke up the bill money. After he finished paying for the car, he got fired from the job, for using drugs on the job. So, I told him to go and find another one I was not giving you a dime. So, life for me took a turn for the worse. He got worse and worse, he started selling his clothes and shoes, he started stealing from the house, and he had lost all dignity and respect for me and himself. Before he lost his job, his friend had convinced him that I was taking his money and giving it to another man. How simple and how weak can one be when all the bills are paid food was always on the table. I started leaving home on Friday nights shutting myself up in the church, fasting and praying for three days and three nights. Through fasting and praying, it gave me the strength and the power to hold on. Time went on and things still did not change. Instead, it got even worse. I went back to the church and shut myself in three more days and three nights, to try to gain the strength and power to try to hold on. I went to church crying every day, an evangelist by the name of Evangelist Larkin came to the house anointed the house, and prayed it seemed to get a little better for a minute. He kept overdosing on drugs and didn't want to go and find another job. He started pimping and playing games. Lest he know that he was only playing games with himself, he wasn't fooling anybody but himself. A lesson to be learned in life as I watched him play with God pretending to want to be saved. As I prayed for him and prayed, he got worse. As time went on, I had to move and move because he kept getting mixed up with the drug dealers, running off with people's drugs, and not paying for them. I had to fast and pray for God to keep the hedge of protection around me so that I wouldn't get killed by him. Because the drug dealers don't care they will kill your whole family. I had been called to the ministry I started laboring on the street corners, going to the nursing homes, and the hospitals laying hands on the sick and they did recover. My first trip on the road was to California. The Lord spoke to me and told me to get the book of bus passes, that you can go anywhere in the world for thirty days. So, I bought the book of bus passes and set out on the Trailways for Los Angeles California. When I got to the bus station in Los Angeles the lord spoke to me and told. me to put my suitcase in a locker, and get on the sunset bus that was parked outside the bus station. So, I got on the bus and rode it down to six and sunset, then I got off, and started walking around, and I saw a woman turn the corner and as she approached me I spoke to her and then I asked her did she know a guy by the name of lucky, but his real name is Leander, she replied that he was her boyfriend, and she told me I look like him and was I his sister, I replied that I was his sister. She said that he was to meet her here in about ten minutes. In about ten minutes he started coming around the corner, she asked me to hide up in the building, so that I could surprise him when he got up there. But he spotted me when he turned the corner, he replied that I looked like his sister, and I replied that I was your sister. He asked me how I found him out here, and what was I doing in LA. I replied that the Lord asked me to come out here and give you a message. I told him that the Lord told me to tell you to come out of LA. I told him I was to stay here for three days, and on the third day, I was to depart for New York City. So, he said that he was going to come later, so I departed. Thirty days later he went to jail for six months. When he got out, he went back to prison for eleven years. So, when the word of the Lord goes out, it shall not return unto him void. So, after he had completed his eleven years he joined me in Dallas Texas. After going on to New York, I headed back home to Chicago. When I got back their death had taken place, my husband's aunt fell dead with an insulin needle in one hand and a bottle of Canadian Club in the other hand. The word of the Lord lets us know that the wedge of sin is death, but the gift of God is eternal life. He had sold all the furniture and everything we had. So, the Lord told me to prepare to leave the city of Chicago and move to Texas. I thought that if I left Chicago my husband would get better, get off the drugs, and turn his life over to the Lord. Surprise he did not, he got worse. But thanks be to God all the fasting and praying I had done came into play when I needed the strength to make it through. My Bishop out of Chicago told me that I was going to leave him on the highway. And that's exactly what I did. It took me about ten years, and I finally had enough. He stole everything, he wouldn't work, and if he worked, he only worked for himself. So, things got rough. So, I left Dallas Texas, and I came to St. Louis, got stuck in St. Louis for a few months, and left there and went into San Francisco.

We were there for one year. And he left again and went to sleep in the streets on Skid Row just to get the drugs and alcohol. He didn't want to do anything with his life, nor did he want to be anybody, what a terrible shame I have got myself mixed up with. So, I decided to leave and I left him right on the streets of San Francisco. One of my youngest sisters gave me her son because she was not mentally able to raise him so I had him with me when I left Chicago. So, he and I packed up and took the bus to Boston Massachusetts. We went into a shelter and they gave us emergency housing. So, I found a babysitter, and I took the bus back into San Francisco to get my stuff out the storage, and I ran into him, I got a traveler's aide to buy him a ticket to Boston and I told him that this would be your last trip if you didn't change and repent. Got to Boston in about two months an earthquake took place and tore up San Francisco. When God tells you to move, you must obey orders. What if I had stayed there, I might not be living right today, this was in November 1988, and the earthquake took place in February 1989. We are here in Boston, and things did not change he robbed the house again, I started doing foster care, and he robbed all the food from the house from the kids, and stole their video games and tapes. A friend of mine gave me a sewing machine that sewed leather, I had it taken to the shop had new wires put on and had it put into a new case, he stole that and pawned it for drugs. The devil had me so mad, that I had to do something because the devil was pushing me to kill him. He did not want to work and kept stealing everything I had worked hard for. We were there for about two years. I had to go to the dentist one day and get a tooth pulled, they had to put me to sleep, he robbed my purse took my Cadillac, and left me at the dentist with no money and no way to get home. I called a cab and borrowed money from the kids to pay the cab driver. We went to the beach he hitched and hiked back home to steal the air compressor set. He climbed up the back stairs, and broke in through the bathroom window, when he saw that it wasn't there, he stole one of the kid's games, and my little niece's birthday suites. So, I started preparing to move back to Dallas, and I left him right on the streets of Boston. We moved to Dallas for four years and I started driving buses, and then we moved again to Dayton Ohio. So, we had contact with him after some years. And he said that he was going to change and gave him one last chance when he got to Dayton. Set him up to go back in training for Culinary Arts, found him a job, and let him borrow seven hundred dollars to purchase him a car, he was to pay me back two hundred dollars every two weeks, until it was paid in full. And he was to pay one hundred every two weeks until he had paid for the car. Well, he tried to fulfill his oath for about one month, and then he changed from Dr. Jekale to Mr. Hyde. So here we go again, he refuses to come back home with the paycheck. I called him and told him to return the car before I called the police and put a warrant on it. So, he took the car went into my bank account, and robbed the church account for over five thousand dollars. I went up to his job, screaming, and told the manager, he was stealing hamburgers, and quarter-pounder hamburgers from McDonald's. They fired him on the spot. I moved out of Trotwood Ohio, and moved over to Xenia. After the move, the Lord spoke to me to go to Dayton and put the warrant on the car, because he claimed someone jumped into the car and took it. So, after we went over to Dayton to put the warrant on the car the Lord spoke to me to go home and pack because he wanted me to go to Chicago and preach for the weekend. We went home packed and got on the road after the children got out of school. In the meantime, I had adopted two more children from Columbus Ohio, and I had my niece from another sister, who had passed away earlier in life. So, we went to Chicago, and preached, left Sunday evening got back early Monday morning, the children got up and went to school, and my mother got up and went over to Dayton to change her address at the Department of Human Services. When we got there, they told us that her worker was not in, but we could wait. We decided to wait, we were there from about ten thirty to about four-thirty. We were in very good spirits even after waiting for so long. After we finished, I told my mother, I said Mom don't you feel something is wrong, we had sat in that place all day, and did not complain at all. She replied yes, when we got outside at our new Windstar, the car that was pawned to the drug dealer was parked in the back of the brand-new Windstar I had a couple of sets of keys, so I jumped in it and took it across the bridge and parked it underground of the transit authority. I locked it down and I left and ran back to the corner, and I met a driver going to the garage, I asked him what time the bus came up on the corner, and he replied I had seven minutes. As I was running back to the corner, I heard the voice of the Lord tell me to watch my back, because my husband was in the area. When I got to the corner, I was so restless I could not be still. The spirit of the Lord turned me around in the front of a top metal place, and there he was, with another man and two prostitutes. I did not recognize him, I asked him if was he said yes, then he asked when was I coming to get him to take him home, I did not answer, he asked repeatedly, so I replied go across the street and sit on that bench, and I'll be right back. As of today, 2017 it has been twenty-five years. I had to put an end to the madness once and for all. I left him sitting right on that bench, right where he should have been left years before that. A dope attic has no love no respect, for you, and nobody else. The only thing they see is their greed for drugs and alcohol. From 1978 until 1998 I prayed and prayed, about that matter, the only thing God kept telling me was that He was the Alpha and the Omega, the beginning and the end, the first and the last, behold I am he that lives and I'm alive forevermore. So now I'm in my forties and the hardest part of the storm is almost over but not yet. I got rid of that problem once and for all so I started raising the four adopted children. How I made it through all those years from the age of nineteen to the age of forty-three, it had to be God, I could have lost my mind, the devil kept trying to get me to kill him. One of the commandments is that Thou shall not kill, so I got rid of him keep from killing him by stealing all the stuff I worked hard for. So, I moved out of Ohio into Indianapolis, then to St. Louis, and then to Tampa Florida, back to St. Louis, and now I'm fifty-eight, my destination is Chicago, back where I started forty years ago. Been in the evangelist field from my twenties until my late fifties, the first half of my journey is over, and know the second half has started. Started driving buses in my twenties getting ready to retire from driving and getting ready to start a home for people with disabilities. And getting ready to build a ministry from the ground up.

CHAPTER-FOUR

THE PRICE YOU PAY FOR NOT HAVING GOD AND EDUCATION

The year I was supposed to graduate I dropped out of high school. I got so depressed, and I was not able to complete my last year. I was not able to focus because of the depression. I dreamed about my graduation, and what I was going to do after my graduation. After falling into depression and not being able to focus, I stopped functioning, like a normal person; I started getting into arguments with my mom every day. Then I just up and stopped going to school. I would lay up in my bed and sleep so that I wouldn't have to face what today may bring me. I didn't want to do anything but sleep, and then I decided to go into Job Corp. Went and signed up and I chose to go to Attu bury Indiana, they shipped me off to Indiana, and I stayed there for six months, I got into trouble and got put out because of my attitude. I met this guy there while I was In Indiana, and he promised me a good life if I moved to Chicago. So, when I left Job Corp, my best friend that was from Chicago. She sneaked me onto the bus I laid down in the back seat and put my coat over my head, pretending like I had been on the bus all alone. I made it to Chicago, and he and his father were waiting for me. I went home with them and I stayed in Chicago for one month. I left Chicago and went back home to East St. Louis and was there for about a year and a half. So, I stayed home all while I was there, and I heard a voice speak to me and it said that, on my 19th birthday I was going to be leaving East St. Louis and were going to Chicago. So, I packed my trunk, and my little brown suitcase, and lived out of that suitcase until my nineteenth birthday. My family said oh you aren't going anywhere; I told them to just wait and see. On my nineteenth birthday February 23rd, 1977 I was at the Greyhound bus station and boarded the bus at twenty-six PM and had about seventy-five dollars in my pocket, after buying my ticket, I only had about forty-five dollars left in my pocket, that's when my mother gave me thirty more dollars to put in my pocket, so that I had seventy-five dollars when I left home. Made it to Chicago my friend was there waiting for me when I got there. I already had a place to go before I got there. After going to Chicago, I had to think about where I was going and what am I going to do. So, I started going and filling out applications. I was there for about a couple of months and things just weren't right everybody around me had dropped out of high school and was using drugs and alcohol. I got very depressed, and when my boyfriend left home, I went into the bedroom and started praying, I asked the Lord to forgive me for all my sins and would you please bless me with a job, because I had no more money and I needed a job. Before I could get up off my knees from praying the telephone rang, and it was someone from the human resource department from Steward and Werner, she asked me if I was still looking for a job, and if so, would I like to come and work for them, and I told them yes. I went in the next day interviewed, and got the job. This was the beginning of miracles for me. I was so happy, until I started asking myself questions, about praying, I was just on my knees praying for a job and before I could get up the phone rang for me a job. So, I started working and discovered that I didn't want to work in factories, so I went down to Malcolm X College to enroll in the GED program and started taking college courses at the same. I took the GED test and missed it by twelve points, I went back and studied again and missed it again by three points, and I went back for the last time and I passed it, I was so happy, and I was persistent that I was going to get my high school diploma and I did. I was still trying to get my associate's degree in Computer Programming, I was doing very well, I had got my GPA, up to 2.79, and then up to 3.0. Then things began to happen, my husband stopped bringing home his paycheck to pay the bills, and I still had another year to go to be able to obtain my associate's degree in Computer programming. So, I dropped out and enrolled in a Computer School, and I took up Computer Operations, which I did graduate with a certificate in Computer Operations. While I was enrolled in the Computer Learning Center, I went out and found another job in a bindery and had to go back to work while I was still in school, because my husband stopped bringing home his paycheck so I didn't know what else to do now. It was very hard work and I hated that job, I complained every day about that job, I worked there for about four years. I then started preparing to move to Dallas Texas. So, I moved to Dallas and started working for Sears as a scanner. So, Sears was talking about going out of business and I knew that I needed to do something, I saw an ad in the newspaper, about training for a school bus driver, so I decided to go down there and fill out an application for Dallas Independent School District. So, when I got down there, they told me that they would train me for a class B commercial driver's license. They told me that I needed a high school diploma or a GED, so I took a copy of it into them and sent it off for my driving record out of Chicago, when I got it back, they hired me, and I started training to be a professional driver. Glory is to God I had gone back to school and received my GED and was able to change the course of my life with the help of God. I trained for about two weeks and, then they took me to a motor vehicle I performed my pre-trip, took my road test, and passed. She told me to work on my breaking and I was going to be just fine. While I'm still trying to better myself, my husband still doesn't want to go back to school to better himself. I was not aware that he had been on drugs ever since he was about fourteen years, dropped out of high school in the tenth grade, I tried to convince him to go and get his GED but he didn't have a mind to do anything. Now, he was addicted to all types of drugs, and so all he wanted to do was to use drugs and to sell drugs, I threatened to leave him if he didn't stop and get himself safe, and go to church and give your life over to

Christ. He promised me that he would, but never did. He started robbing and stealing from our home, and robbing our home until it got unbearable. I continued living for God even though the life I had with this man became impossible to live with. I didn't want to work in a factory all my life, because I hated that kind of work, standing up for hours, my hands and feet started hurting. My husband had to go back and forth to various jobs because he didn't have a high school diploma. He works a while and gets fired for stealing from his job, and for using drugs on the job, that is the price you should pay for not having an education, and for not having Christ in your life. He became very angry with me because I chose not to follow him in the things that he had got his self-caught up in. So, he stole everything in the house, and then he refused to be sorry about it, he blamed me for him being the way he was. So, I had to start choosing to keep him and keep trying to get him some help, well on down the road I figured out that he didn't want to go to school, and he didn't want Jesus, so my choice was that I must leave him about this time nineteen eighty-four he was too far gone. When I started for Dallas, I was already called into the ministry, so I got rid of him and continued to work for the Lord. He ended up homeless, with no job, and no place to go. He ended up sleeping under the bridge because he robbed our house and he had no one to turn to. As I started the ministry, I had never seen so many people sleeping under the bridge, and homeless in all the days of my life. So, we would cook up big meals, and set up tables to feed the ones that were under the bridge, and had nowhere to go. The very next day we saw the same people back under the bridge again, and this was day after day. They had even found old mattresses and set them up under the bridge so that they could have a place to rest after they had eaten. I didn't understand but my heart started to let me understand, as I began to see that if school and the books and God don't' teach you a lesson, the streets will, you have to determine which one of these you want to learn a lesson from. Most of them couldn't read and write, because they dropped out of school early. So, if you can't read and write, you can't fill out an application, so therefore you are not capable of filling out a job application, to be able to go out and get yourself a job to be able to be a productive citizen, in life. You are not capable of getting a job, when you are addicted to drugs and alcohol. When you are addicted to drugs and alcohol you don't have a mind to get up and go and get a job, because you are not in your right mind. I remember back when they started doing drug testing for drugs and alcohol testing, by this time it was so many people had gotten addicted to these drugs and alcohol that it was not funny. I started feeling sorry for those people who were out there addicted to drugs and alcohol, and homeless and with no place to go and no one to turn to. This is the price you pay for not having an education, and being addicted to controlled substances, and the price you must pay for not having Christ in your life. You are just out there, and it was such a frightening thing to see so many people homeless and addicted to drugs and alcohol, and not have Christ. This was the very thing that I was afraid of when I first left home, and moved to Chicago, was the very reason I accepted Christ into my life, it started taking place not too many years after I got saved. Until you decide that you want help for your addiction you will forever be out there. You are going to have to acknowledge that you are helpless and that you need help, and then you are going to have to ask for help, the Lord is standing watching and waiting for you to ask him for help. You're lost without God, not only lost in this world but you are lost spiritually and in the natural as well. You can't go to work and make a living for yourself. A good percentage of people when they drop out of high school start having children, don't further their education, can't support their children, because they don't have jobs, and then they end up getting state and federal assistance, which includes medical, cash assistance, plus food stamps. Know you are not able to support your children you are dependent upon the state to provide for you and your children. I have seen down through the years that in some families a pattern is followed, grandmother was on state and federal assistance, mother was on federal and state assistance, and now your children are having children and on federal and state assistance. And, if the grandmother was on drugs and alcohol, the children end up being on drugs and alcohol, and their children end up being on drugs and alcohol. It's called a generational curse, down the bloodline. After dropping out of high school having children, and starting receiving public assistance, it goes down the bloodline, from generation to generation. Somewhere down the line, the cycle must be broken. And sometimes with this young generation drugs and alcohol are all they know, because of their family history. The cycle goes on and on until someone breaks that generational curse. There is a high price you must pay for not having Christ and education in your life. Homelessness is one of the prices you must pay for not having an education, and not being able to care for your children, you must depend upon the state for assistance to be able to pay your bills and to put clothes on the children's backs. The government put you through so much stuff to be able to receive assistance from the federal government, that includes standing in a long line, and being there for a whole day. Imagine having a high school diploma and a college degree, you wouldn't have to worry about how you are going to feed your children, and if they get sick, you wouldn't have to worry about medical help for them, food and clothes would be no problem for you and the children. These things are necessities for us to have to be productive citizens in society. And if we don't have these things, how are we to teach our children how to obtain these things, and get an education, so that they do not have to come down the road that you came down, and go through the things that you had to go through, and to be able to get a good job so that they would not have to depend upon the state and the federal government for assistance…If we don't have education how are we to tell our children to go and get an education when we don't have any? It is a very hard thing when we must depend upon the state and the federal government, for our cash assistance, medical, and food stamps, to pay our bills. The government only gives your assistance only once a month, your bills succeed the amount of assistance the federal government gives you. If you run short during the month, you are just out of luck, because the government only provides for you once a month. Why not sacrifice and go back and get your GED so that you can be successful and have what you want, and be able to give your children some of the things that they and, and be able to provide a wee nurturing healthy lifestyle for your children. You should also pursue a college degree for yourself and your children, so that the children may be able to follow in your footsteps to have an education and to be able to have s successful and productive lifestyle. With God and education, you don't have to wait once a month for a stimulus payment from the federal government to provide food and clothes for the children. The reason why it is so easy to get an education so that the government won't have to dictate to you how to spend your own money. And especially you don't have to let someone dictate to you how much you get and when you get it. Some people get caught up in the system, until they get comfortable, and become so dependent upon the system that they get lazy, and don't want to go out and get a job. After the federal government started aiding the people who weren't capable of making a living for themselves, they got so dependent upon the system that the cash assistance wasn't enough for them to meet their needs for the entire month, so they started selling the food stamps to people that had very good paying jobs. Most of the people that were selling the food stamps were on drugs and alcohol. They were abusing drugs and alcohol to the point where they could not pay their bills, nor could they provide housing and food for their children. The government didn't give you the assistance for you to abuse the system, and allow you to neglect your children, and end up being homeless, for nonpayment of rent. It was given to you for a short period, to give you a chance to better yourself. The food stamps were for you to put food on the table for your children. The government expected you to provide an adequate place for you and your children to have a place to live and pay your bills. So many have abused and misused the food stamp system, until now the whole country is in a deficit. We have never in our entire life seen so many people addicted to drugs and alcohol, to a point where people have taken the food stamps cash assistance and used it for drugs and alcohol. And were addicted to the point where they couldn't provide for their children and the state had to step in and put the children into foster care, and gave them a certain amount of time to go to parenting classes and attend drug and alcohol rehabilitation programs. Most of them that lost their children due to drug and alcohol abuse, never went back to get their children. We have never seen so many children in foster care, and up for adoption, in all the days of our lives. So many grandparents had to step in and take their grandchildren to stop them from going to the state. But there were so many that didn't have any relatives to take them so they went up to the state and then went up for adoption because of the abuse and neglect. Every time you go to the grocery store you have so many people waiting at the store, or walking around the store asking you if you want to buy any food stamps. After abusing and misusing the food stamps selling them for cash to be able to get the drugs and alcohol, and now a few days later they don't have any groceries, don't pay their bills, and the children don't have food to eat for the whole month. Their habit was more important than their children and their bills. So, what do they do they go around the community and find out what days each church gives out free food, know they are at the food pantry, trying to get week-old food for them and their children to eat. They end up hitting every food pantry in town, to have food. Why would you want day-old food when you could have had fresh food directly from the grocery store? They also go and stand in line at the community action agency to get their lights and gas bills paid, when the state has given them the assistance to pay their bills and not to let the bills be disconnected because they have misused the funds that were given to them. They used to have agencies that paid your rent if you had an eviction notice. Why do you have to put yourself through all of this when you can get up and go and get an education for yourself? You might feel like it may be too late, but it's never too late, if you have health and strength in your body, and are enclosed within your right mind it is never too late for you to go and get yourself an education. After the government started putting stipulations on the number of benefits you can receive and a time limit on how long you can receive them, the devil gave the people another loophole to be able to deceive the system, by pretending to have certain types of problems and being unable to work to able to get on SSI, then they started abusing those funds, by abusing drugs and alcohol. After they got their SSI going, they started taking their children to the doctor pretending that the children were ADHD or had psychological problems and had the doctors putting them on medication that they did not need. So that was another loophole satin set people up for to be able to get more money for more drugs and alcohol. If you follow a pattern of unrighteousness to lie and to deceive, to get what you want without working for it, you will forever be bound, you must have a desire to come off drugs and alcohol, most people that are bound by drugs, and alcohol, don't come off them until something bad happens or until they get into bad health from using so much of it. You will forever be homeless strung out if you don't recognize that you have a problem. Therefore, it is so important for you to go to school get an education, and get Christ in your life so that you won't be bound out there in a world of sin. Find a church home get with the elders of the church start praying, encourage yourself allow God to pick you up, and carry you into a better place. I was determined not to let the Devil take me there that lifestyle presented itself to me but I turned it down, I went the road God had called me to go down at the age of nineteen, I had a choice, and I chose what I thought would be best for me because I had dreams as a child, I visualize what my house would be like when I was a child, because I was the child out of thirteen children who always did the interior decorating for my mom, and I enjoyed painting and putting up wallpaper all over the house. When I got to Chicago, I refused to let the devil take me down a road of drugs and alcohol and to be caught up in poverty. We know that drugs and alcohol lead you into poverty. Poverty is the main cause of crime that's in the world today. The robbing the stealing, and the killing are because of the drug abuse that has taken over the world. After you have been on drugs for so long you can't go out and get a job, that's when you start robbing killing, and stealing to get that fix. You don't care who you rob, or who you kill if you get the next fix. Some so many men and women are addicted to drugs and alcohol, and are homeless, and sleep under bridges, and in homeless shelters, because they have robbed their families, until their families have disowned them, and have banded them from coming to their home because you cannot be trusted into nobody's home. So therefore, you must go to the homeless shelter or get a bed under the bridge, to be able to go somewhere and rest. If you get a chance to get a bed at the shelter, you must be there in line at a certain time for you to be able to get a bed for tonight. When you get to a point in life where you have to go and sleep under the bridge or go stand in the soup line to be able to eat and sleep, I think that it's time for you to call upon the name of Jesus, it should be a wakeup call to turn your will over to the Lord, knowing that you can't change anything, the word of the Lord say's Not by power, Nor by might, But it's by his spirit say's the Lord. In the thirty-six years I have been safe, I have seen so many addicted and have become comfortable with that lifestyle until they don't want to come out. I have seen them go all day hunting up soda pop cans cash them in get the change and buy drugs and alcohol with it. I have never seen one person who was addicted to drugs buy any food to eat, that's because drugs and alcohol were more important to them than eating. Some have been in and out of rehabilitation, and still didn't come off the drugs and alcohol, they came right out and went right back out there and started doing the same thing they were doing before they went in. That's because they are not ready to stop doing what they are doing. And most of them get caught up in the system, and some end up going to prison for a long time, because of the crimes they have committed to get the drugs. I've seen some go to prison for a long time and when they got out; they started doing the same thing they were doing before they went to prison. After we reach a certain age, we should have come out of childhood. I'm reminded of the Apostle Paul when he said when I was a child I spoke as a child, I acted like a child, but when I became a man, I had to put away childish things. When you get to a point in life as to be your family disowns you, you ought to hurry as fast as you can and get to God because you can't live in this life alone. God has already told us to seek him where he may be found, and call upon him while he is near, let the wicked man forsake his way, and the unrighteous man forsake his thoughts. Most people who abuse drugs and alcohol, usually have a self-esteem problem or end up in a situation where they were abused somewhere down the line. You just don't start abusing drugs and alcohol for no apparent reason, you figure the more you get high you don't have to remember anymore, but I'm here to tell you when the high is gone, the problem is still there, you are only bringing self-destruction upon your body, because if you sow to the flesh you are going to reap corruption. You must come to grips with yourself and give whatever problem you are having over to the lord because he is the only one who can fix it, and the only one who can give you peace of mind behind whatever situation you find yourself in. You must also forgive the abuser, and after forgiving them you must forgive yourself, and then find yourself under repentance before God. Once you look back and find out what the problem is that caused you to go down that road, it can be corrected, if you just allow the Lord Jesus Christ to fix it for you. You are going to have to love yourself because if you don't learn to love yourself you will never be able to break free from the hand of the enemy. If you can't love yourself, you definitely can't have love for anybody else, it's impossible to love anybody, and most of all you will never love anybody if you don't break free from bondage. So, therefore, you must live day to day without a care in the world for yourself and anybody else. Some things in life may be meant for us to go through, for our learning, but that doesn't mean for you to stay into whatever God has allowed you to go through, somewhere down the line you must break free, from the yoke of bondage. I started preaching at the age of twenty-one, I could go to quite a few large cities, and the way other young people were living I let that be my guide not to go down that road, I didn't want to be homeless I enjoyed going home to a nice warm bed after working hard all day, and after being out on the road preaching. I decided early in life on the road I was going to take I'm so glad that God gave me a mind as to where I can think for myself, and not let anybody lead me down a path of no return, so many went down the wrong path and never got a chance to get off that path and get on the right path. Who knows once you get on the wrong road, you will be able to turn and get back on the right road. I saw in my early twenties that being on the wrong road, you could even lose your very life on that road, and I didn't want to take that chance and end up dying out of Christ, it was just too risky for me. Growing up with thirteen children in our household, we have never been homeless, nor have we ever had our utilities cut off. I give myself the highest praise because she tried and she had done a wonderful job being a single mom with no one to help. So, when I became an adult, the fear was great upon me until I didn't want to be homeless, I didn't want to know what being homeless felt like. So, I made that choice to go to school, get an education get a job, and stay with the Lord, so that I could become a productive citizen in the community. I had even met people who had college degrees but had gone down the wrong road with drugs and alcohol and ended up under the bridge, and some were never able to get back off that path. Once you get out there and you end up not having a desire to come out of that lifestyle, you are in a world of trouble. You never want it to be said it's too late. If you have health and strength in your body, you have a chance to correct yourself but once you are dead you can't undo anything, it is too late.

He that hath an ear, let him hear
What the spirit said unto the Churches:
Revelation 3:6

THE PRICE YOU PAY
FOR HAVING GOD AND
EDUCATION

As you know, I can testify for myself, that there is a reality in serving a true and a living God. You must have that experience to be able to testify to this. As I started at the age of nineteen, I started with nothing and I had to grow into something. I chose to grow into that which was right and righteous. The path you choose that's what you must live with for the rest of your days. I stepped out on faith when I left East, St. Louis Illinois at the age of nineteen. It was kind of scary, although a very dear friend of mine had a place set up for me to come, that was a blessing in itself. Got my GED accumulated credit hours in Computer science and completed one year of learning how to operate all the input-output devices, and learn how to operate all the hardware and software. And graduated. Started driving commercial vehicles, and in 2000 started a truck driving school and completed that possessing a class A with all the endorsements. In 2001 went back to Sinclair College and got my Real-Estate Degree. And got my appraisal certificate. Now I have e few things I can do along the way. Adopted four children, and now they have their own children. One is a nurse, one is an engineer, and one got a four-year free ride to the University of Indianapolis, and majored in accounting, and know he is the auditor for the city of Indianapolis. I also have close to sixty hours in computer science, which I'm getting ready to use to go back to school to major in accounting. I'm getting ready to retire from driving the buses and trucks and getting ready to purchase land so that I can put down single-family module homes for people with disabilities. And I'm getting ready to build a ministry from the ground up, I have been in the evangelist field for thirty-seven years. Had a job in every city I went in. Learning how to operate motor coaches and transit buses, I could find a job very quickly in every city I went in. I also started school again in Dayton, Ohio for Business Administration. So, now I can take those credit hours into accounting and get my accounting degree so that I can be able to manage my finances and payroll. It's going on forty years now, God has never left me or forsaken me. He has told us in his word that he would be with us through thick and thin. He let us know that he would never leave us or forsake us, and I can truly testify to his words. He's a God that cannot lie neither is he the son of man that he should repent, if he said it, he shall perform just what his word has said. I only had two more semesters to have my associate's degree in computer science. Things in the marriage got so bad that I got depressed because my husband stopped bringing his paycheck home to pay the bills. I dropped out and went to a trade school for computer operations for a year and I did graduate. I had to find a job in the meantime while I finished this year. For all the good jobs I had, I had to have a high school diploma. Most of my jobs were driving for the transit authorities in the different states I went in to preach. I don't think that I would have gone this far in life without God. I would have never accumulated what I have accumulated if it had not been for me going back to school and getting an education that led to being able to get these good jobs from the state, driving commercial vehicles. In life having God and education along with it brings forth happiness and joy. When I'm able to pay my bills I'm at peace with myself, therefore it is so important to go to school so that you don't have to depend upon government assistance. They dictate how much you should have once a month, anybody in their right mind would not wait on a check one time out of the month, and food stamps for you and your children once a month. I grew up on a once-a-month check and food stamps once a month. My mother was receiving food stamps once a month and government assistance once a month. We always ran out of food the last week of the month, and my mom had to sell some of the food stamps to be able to pay all the bills for the whole month. I saw her struggle; I always had a sad spirit for my mom. I told her when I was grown, I would be back to help her and help her with the other children that she had left to grow. Even when we ran out of food the last week of the month, we went and walked the neighborhood to find pop bottles. Back in the sixties and the seventies, pop bottles were five cents, and then they increased to ten cents a bottle. We had found enough to get at least five to six dollars off the pop bottles. And then sometimes we would trade them in go back and get them and trade them in for the second time. And then the people at the store got wise and they started marking the bottles across with a black magic marker. So, we took some alcohol wiped the bottles off, and traded the same bottles back in again. We could buy beans and rice chicken backs and chicken necks and corn meal to make bread to go with the beans and rice. We also had money left to buy a bag of popcorn for all of us before bedtime. My mom went back to school as soon as she had the thirteen kids, and she also got a part-time job around the corner, at the neighborhood store. As I grew up, I realized how important it was for us to go to school and get an education, because our childhood was the best as anyone can expect it to be. We did not want to grow up like our mom with all those children and end up on welfare. Out of thirteen children, only two did not complete high school and did not go to college. One boy and one girl. My mom struggled to get us through high school and struggled to see to us finishing. I desired to never go through what my mom had to go through; it was very tough. When my mom went back to school, she got her GED and then she went on to state community college and got an Associate's degree in auto mechanics then when she graduated, she went back again and got another associate's degree in teaching. So, now she has two degrees. She used her auto mechanic Degree to fix her cars and she even taught the boys how to fix cars. Then she worked as a teacher until she died in 2005. She could go to work and support the last eight children on an earned income, instead of continuing welfare. She had told us many times not to have all those children, and go to school and get an education so that we would not have to depend upon the welfare system. Out of thirteen children, only one ended up on welfare and refused to go and get an education until President Bill Clinton put an end to being on welfare your entire life. So, she had no other choice but to find a job go to work, and stop depending upon the federal government to take care of you and your children. I have also completed thirty- seven years in the ministry, and almost forty years being saved, walking with God for almost forty years has been a great experience. It has been an experience of a lifetime; I wouldn't take anything for the journey that I have had with the Lord. The life I have had is getting better and better. Life brings about a change. One more year I'll be sixty years of age, I feel the same as I did when I was in my twenties. My youth has been restored as the eagle. My mom always preached to us not to go out and have all those kids like she did. She constantly reminded us of her mistake. Every day of her life she often talked about it, and it made her very depressed. When our father left, she labored to take care of us, and I never heard her complain about taking care of us. My heart was so heavy feeling sorry for her. I tried to do whatever I could to help her until some of us got out of the way. As time rolled on things became a little easier for all of us. We didn't miss our dad a lot, because of the domestic violence that took place in the home. We woke up every night screaming and crying because our dad jumped on our mother every night, he comes home drunker than a skunk. Fighting all the time, he only did it at night when he thought everyone was asleep. Well, we were asleep until he woke us up, and tried to make us help him jump on our mother. When he tried to make me slap my mom, I told him that it was not the right thing to do, and I did not obey him. Mom regretted many days of marrying that man. After she went back to school and got her education, she became quite proud of herself. She finally started being happy with herself. Fortunately, we did not end up with all those children, because we saw what she went through, and we did not want to be on welfare and food stamps. When we got grown, we went straight to work. I'm in my late fifties and I don't have any children. I raised two of my sister's children. In which one had passed away early. And she did finish high school, and went on to college, but she did not complete it. The reward you have for having God and education. I'm now in the process of retiring from driving for thirty-one years. Getting ready to open up a home for people with disabilities, and also starting a ministry.

CHAPTER-FIVE

THE BENEFITS OF WISDOM THROUGH OBEDIENCE

Proverbs 4:7

King James Version

Wisdom is the principle thine: Therefore, get wisdom: And with all thy getting, get an understanding.

Proverb 4:8

Exalt her and she shall promote thee; She shall bring thee to honor, when thou do embrace her.

At the age of nineteen, I moved from East St. Louis Ill, to Chicago, Ill. I had visited the city one time, and I decided to move here when I turned nineteen years of age. I was seventeen years old when I visited here. I was in Job Corps in Atterbury Indiana. I end up getting put out for fighting. Me and my best friend I called Pepper. She already lived in the Chicago area. I didn't want to go back to East St. Louis Ill. I was having a really hard time getting along with my mother. So, I sneaked on the Greyhound bus in Indianapolis, Indiana, and pretended like I was sleeping already on the bus, and I got away with a free ride to Chicago. When I got put out of Job Corps, I had a one-way ticket to East St. Louis, and I didn't want to go back there. After rerouting myself to Chicago I stayed there for a month and then I went home. After making it into Chicago I called up the guy I had met there, and he and his father picked me up at the bus station. So, I waited until I turned nineteen years of age, packed my bags left East St. Louis, and moved permanently to Chicago on my birthday. I had been so depressed living in that town because I knew that I could not be what I wanted to be there. There was no hope, nor where there a future for me there. When I got here in Chicago, I found a job, and then I went back to school to get my GED. I enrolled in Malcolm X Community College and started working on my GED and I started my major which was computer science. I enjoyed working with computers. And in the meantime, I started going to church and I got saved, and filled with the gift of the Holy Ghost. As I got saved my eyes came open. The scriptures let us know that in much wisdom is much grief. I escaped a lot of pain and agony in my life. The obedience to God, allowed me to bypass death and destruction at an early age. Obedience to God also helped me to escape being addicted to drugs and alcohol at an early age. For this is the benefit of wisdom through obedience. God has also blessed to not to have children out of wedlock. Many people were not as fortunate as me, because they didn't want to listen. And when you are in a position where nobody can tell you anything you are in a bad frame of mind. Throughout our lives, we should constantly be learning. No matter how old we get, there ought to be somebody out there who should be able to tell us something. Are giving us direction, in the way that we should go. After getting saved at the age of nineteen, I was fortunate to be around elders who were in their sixties and seventies. So, therefore I was very fortunate to be around them. They taught me the way of Holiness. It was very tough in my twenties being saved. But I held on and know I'm in my sixties, and I am so blessed to be here in perfect health, and in my right frame of mind, with no addictions. Because of my obedience as a young adult, God has added years to my life. And therefore, I am so grateful unto the highest for his love and kindness unto me and for the grace and mercy that he has shown me. Therefore, at the age of seventeen God had given me my first set of instructions. At the age of nineteen

I started carrying them out. That was forty-two years ago. After I got here my next set of instructions was to find me a church home and start going to church. For I heard the voice of God saying that If I find me a church to go to, he will shield me and protect me as to where no one will ever bother me again. And I carried those instructions out. My next set of instructions was to go back to school get my GED and start college. And I carried those instructions. These instructions came directly from God. I don't care who doesn't believe it I started praying at an early age and I have seen miracle after miracle. I wouldn't have come this far If I hadn't believed that there was someone greater than me who was leading me and guiding me down the road that I should go. One thing that I know is that man cannot steer you and guide you down a righteous path. The devil has instructions for you too. And his instructions don't consist of anything righteous. You wonder how to distinguish between the voice of the Lord and the voice of the devil. God will always direct you to do righteous things, but Satan will always give you instructions that will go against the word of the Lord. His instructions are not Godly, nor are they righteous, they will always be against the word of God. Wisdom promises safety. For faith in God knows no defeat. You are only defeated when you start obeying the voice of Satan. When you go against righteousness, you sin against your soul. KJV: Ezekiel 18:4

Behold, all souls are mine; as the soul of the father, so is the soul of the son is mine: the soul that sins, shall die. You cannot have a prosperous life without the proper instructions. We need instructions in this life. Wisdom will bring you into prosperity. AS I can speak about my own life what if I had not obeyed the first two sets of instructions that were given to me? I do not want to imagine where I would be today, or what I would be like right now at the age of sixty- one. I escaped death at an early age, through obedience, which brought me to life. I was called unto the Ministry at the age of twenty- one. I answered the call and began to grow in grace. Two years later at the age of twenty-three, I started in the Evangelist field. My first trip was to L California. I bought a Greyhound pass that lasted thirty days. The Lord spoke to me to go to LA and give my oldest brother a message. And that message was to tell him to come out of LA right now. So, when I got on the Greyhound bus, it took me three days to get there. When I arrived there the Lord told me to put my bags in a locker, go outside get on the Sunset Blvd. bus, and ride it down to Seventh Street, so I followed those instructions and got off on Seventh Street.

I went to the north side of the street and I just waited. I waited about fifteen minutes and this woman was coming around the corner the Lord spoke to me again and told me to ask the woman did she knew a guy by the name of Lucky. When she approached me, I stopped her and asked her did she knew a guy by the name of Lucky, and I told her that his real name was Leander Scruggs, she replied are you his sister, I replied that I was, then she replied that she was his old lady and that she was to meet him right here on this corner in about fifteen minutes. In about fifteen minutes here he comes pimping around the corner. She told me to stand back up inside the building so that we could surprise him when he got up there. As he approached, he began to tell the lady friend of his that I looked just like his sister. I walked out of the building and I said surprise I am your sister. He was so shocked he couldn't believe how I found him. For one thing that stands assured God knows everything about you, he even knows the number of strands that you have on your head.

If I ascend into heaven, thou art there: if I make my bed in hell, behold thou are there.

KJV: Psalms139:9 KJV: Psalms 139:8
If I take the wings of the morning and dwell in the uttermost parts of the sea;
KJV: Psalms 139:10
Even there shall thy hand lead me, and thy right hand shall hold me.

After being in LA for three days, I told my brother that the Lord sent me here to tell you to come out of LA. I carried out the instructions that the Lord had given me, so he said he was coming out but not right now. So, on the third day in the morning, I left the hotel got back on the Greyhound bus, and headed to New York City to carry out more instructions. So, after I got back to Chicago, I packed my bags and moved out of the city to Dallas, Texas. In the meantime, I got a call from my mother my brother went to jail for six months. When he got out, he went back to prison for eleven years. He speaks about that situation right to this day. If I had listened and left when you came there, I wouldn't have gotten caught up in the system the way I did.

This is the benefit of wisdom, to know what's going to happen before it happens. Because of instructions from God, I have avoided many traps and snares that the enemy had plotted to lay before me. And as I look back down through the years, I was so blessed not to get caught up in the tricks and snares of satin. I have traveled over the country for forty years preaching and teaching God's word. It has been a joy to my soul, and strength to my inner man to keep pressing toward the mark of the prize, of a high calling that's in Christ Jesus.

This is the importance of serving God while you are young. Because you can hear God more; and clearer and you don't know any better, but to obey that one voice. And when you are young you are so eager to learn, and you are very quick to hear, that's because you have not gotten a chance to be set in your way as of yet. Don't you see God caught hold of me when I had just reached adulthood? I had not gotten a chance to hit the streets and learn the things of the world as of yet. And I am so grateful to God that he called me and chose me from the foundation of the world. I am glad that he didn't allow me to adapt to the things of this world. Because the more you experience the things of this world it's hard to give some of those things up. I had not tasted the world yet, and I am so glad that I didn't. When God called me, I came. I didn't have anything to give up because I had not experienced anything yet. So, I do believe that the less you know when you are young, the easier it is for God to teach you his way, and his way is the way of holiness.

Solomon affirms here that "in much wisdom is much grief, and he who increases knowledge increases sorrow". However, Proverbs asserts that "Happy is the man who finds wisdom, and the man who gains understanding. **Proverbs: 3:13 KJV**

CHAPTER-SIX

THE PRICE YOU PAY FOR BEING OBEDIENT

But if thou shalt indeed obey his voice and do all that I speak; then I would be an enemy unto thine enemies, and an adversary union thine adversary.

Exodus:23:22

Sometimes it seems to be so hard for us to obey, leadership authority. But as we look around in life, we can see who obeys, and who doesn't. Being obedient will bring you into the power of knowledge, and great riches. I'm still reminded of myself when I got grabbed in the city of Chicago and got away, I heard the voice of the Lord as he instructed me. And as I obeyed his voice, I came out of the situation like he told me I would. After that, he told me to find me a church home to go to and I did. Then he told me that if I found a church to go to, he would shield me and protect me, and no one would ever touch me again. So, after I got in church, I had an older friend living in the building we exercise every, so she gave me a ten-dollar bill to pick her up some oranges. So, I didn't go out for a couple of days, and I thought I better go and get her some and take her the change I told her. Left out of the house it was dark, and I got to the store, changed the ten-dollar bill, and purchased the oranges. When I left the store I had My little coin purse with my bible in it, as I went across the street, a man started coming up in the back of us, and I heard the voice of God say that man was going to try to take your purse. The Lord spoke to me again and said Don't go any further, stand right at this fence and hold on to it. The man came up in the back of me and said keep walking, and I dais for what, he said you see what I have in my hands don't you? So, he asked do you have any money, I pulled my bible out and showed him the word of God. I told him that's all I have, he took off and ran, and never pursued after me. That was the promise of God he had given me when he asked me to start going to church. It's been forty-one years now and no one has ever tried to rob me since. That is God's promise to me to be obedient. And Samual said, hath the Lord as great delight in burnt offerings and sacrifice, as in obeying the voice of the Lord? Behold, to obey is better than the fat of rams.

CHAPTER-SIX-CONTINUES

Honor thy father and thy mother, that thy days may be long upon the land, which the Lord thy God giveth thee. KJV.

Proverbs 20:12

We know that in the last days, perilous times are coming. To be disrespectful, and just plain o mean will lead you down a road of no return. God has given you a home as a child not for you to tell the parents what to do. The parents are to tell you and show you how you should go. And for them to leave you down the road so that you might grow up to be a blessing to yourself and a blessing to others. Many of us who have been taught in the word of God, and have been trained up in the church have no excuse. For as much is given, for much is required. It's time for us to seek the Lord for our salvation, and to seek him with our whole heart. There is a great price we have to pay when we have been instructed and fail to follow the instructions that the Lord has given our elders to give to us. We all are not perfect, because if we were, Jesus wouldn't have to come down from heaven to redeem us. So, therefore we have come short of being perfect. I have made plenty of mistakes. I didn't just sit there and wallow in the mistake, I got right back up and repented, and started all over again. You don't keep doing the same old thing over and over again, that means you are not paying attention, and you are not following orders. You have to stay with the Lord so that you may be able to get it right. Therefore, in our learning, we have something to tell someone else who's found in the same position that we were once in. When we fail to follow instructions when asked to go to school and do our best to finish high school, and we choose to go to the front door of the school, and leave out the back door doing our thing, hanging in the streets, on the street corners, with our gang banging friends, smoking weed, and using drugs, and drinking alcohol, there is a price you pay for being disobedient. Being disobedient has consequences. And the consequences for being disobedient are almost unbearable. I started traveling over the country at the age of twenty-one. I have seen so many people sleeping on the streets, under the bridge, they have a mattress with all their belongings with them in their little corner. It is so sad, that every time I see them, I can't do anything but pray and grieve for them. I have had a chance to minister to many of them. But it's up to them to go and seek help so that they can come out of that situation, of being homeless, having no job, on drugs and alcohol. Get up every morning to panhandle on the same corner for years. They have the same old clothes that they had on last year or the year before. I drive the city bus, I have been driving the city buses for thirty-one years, and one situation that caught my attention, when I was driving the bus in Chicago, I had the Cottage Grove route, a mind had been sleeping under the bridge, for so long, and the city came in under the bridge with the garbage truck, they cleaned up so much garbage that had got piled up from the ground to the top of the bridge, food garbage, clothes, trash mattresses, and they made the man get his coat and leave. And the city department of health came with the garbage people. About two days later he returned and started piling garbage back up again, so the city and the health inspectors came again with the garbage truck, and made him leave again. So, he left they cleaned it back up, and about two days later he was back there again. The situation is still going on. There are consequences you have to pay for being disobedient, whether you are saved or unsaved. I believe you suffer more if you do not have God and education. When you are saved you know how to call on God, and seek him for the things that you need, and also the things that you desire to have. Without God, you can do nothing, and without God, your life will fail. Or as much is given, for much is required. When you know to do good and do it not, to him it is a sin. The more you know. the more you are going to be held accountable for what you do know. I can remember times when I was led not to do something, did not follow my first mind, and did it anyway, there was a price I had to pay for being disobedient. I had to pray my way through and wait for the Lord to come and deliver me from that situation that I got myself into. It was not a good feeling when I disobeyed the leading of the Lord not to do that. Sometimes I didn't get delivered right away, it took some months to get back my peace, for being disobedient. I remember when I had so many problems at home with my mom, I quit school and went to Job-Corp. It worried me so bad when I dropped out of school, I didn't have a piece of mind. I went to Job Corps for six months and got put out of there for fighting. Went back home very depressed, tried to get back in high school, and they told me I had to go to night school to get my GED. I moved to Chicago at the age of nineteen and I started going to Malcolm X College got my GED, and I was enrolled in college, majoring in Computer science. My GPA was 3.79 I got married too young to a man who had already been on drugs. You see what can happen when you don't follow the instructions that have been given to you. One good thing that happened to me for not obeying orders was that I didn't have to be bothered with children. I never had any. Down the road two of my sisters had children and I ended up raising them, and I adopted two from Columbus Ohio. I took them to church had them repent and be baptized, and I taught them the word of God. One of them ended up staying out in the streets all night, and she went to school the next day, I got the police to escort her out of her classroom and I took her down to the court in Dayton Ohio, and I left her with the judge. She wanted to scream at me in my house and talk crazy to me and I told her she had one more time to open her mouth to me and she was going to be on the judge's doorstep. She was only thirteen years of age. When she saw where she was headed, she fell out on the floor of the courthouse, screaming and crying, I told her this was her choice, and she had to live with that. You do not play games with grown folks. There is a price you have to pay for being disobedient. And she played that price from the age of thirteen until she was eighteen, she now has three children with no husband, raising the children on her own, with no help. She is trying to go to nursing school at the age of thirty, and work, and take care of three children on her own. That's the price you have to pay for not having God and education. Keep in mind the price you have to pay for being disobedient, and not willing to accept the instructions that have been given to you. I had my niece and her brother, pull the same trick he was fifteen, and my niece was sixteen. Left home and didn't go to school, The sheriff picked the boy up, he lied and told the sheriff I was going to kill them, they immediately became the word of the state. So, my niece came home and I took her down there where they were holding him and I left both of them and I didn't even look back. The boy went on to school and finished and got a scholarship for academics and graduated from college. My niece quit as soon as she got put into foster care. I made sure that they couldn't get hold of me again. I left Indianapolis and went to Florida drove the bus and was in Disney World free of choice every day. My niece now has five children by different men, no job, no education and she make it look like she is the happiest person in the world with five kids no job, and profess to be a working stay-at-home mom. Who are you fooling, yourself? That's the price you have to pay for not having God and education and the consequences you pay for being disobedient. I refused to go on in life without my high school diploma, my contours would not let me rest until I got my high school diploma. My mom preached to us all the time I want you all to get grown finish high school, and go on to college or a trade school. Know I look back and see what would have happened to me if I hadn't gone back and gotten my high school diploma. I saw so many people under the bridge and sleeping on the street who didn't finish high school, and again I saw people who had finished high school strung out on drugs and alcohol and did not want to go any further. So, they are out on the corner with a cup panhandling every day. They have a certain time they get there and a certain time they leave, and the next day they start it all back over again. This goes on for years and years. The first thing they ask for is money so that they can buy some food, and I saw people give them food they get so mad because they wanted the money instead of the food. This is the price you pay for not wanting to go to school and get an education so that you might be profitable in life to yourself and others. Rebellion is the sin of witchcraft. And as you go on in life in your way and no one can tell you anything, the worse you will get. Some get tired of themselves and suicide crepes in and of them are successful and some are not so successful. As I started growing into a teenager, I had a stumbling block that was put in my way where I suffered from depression. And after I left home, I was able to go back to school and get my high school diploma. People don't realize that the battle is not with flesh and blood, but the warfare is in the mind. You have to continue to pray and warfare in your mind because that's where the devil attacks you at the most. I had to learn how to warfare in the spirit realm to keep my mind protected at all costs. Suppose I had let everything I was going through with my mom get the best of me. I would no doubt be out there in the streets, on drugs and alcohol, and under the bridge sleeping, begging for money to buy food. I had to overcome lots of obstacles, and still have a lot more to overcome. Because the more you learn, the more you will be held accountable for. Solomon says in much wisdom is much grief. There is a battle going on in everybody's mind, you have to figure out whether you are going to fight in the battle, or go on in life and accept being defeated. If you choose not to fight then you have already lost the battle before it started, you chose not to fight back. This is why so many people choose to use drugs and alcohol, because of the battle that's waring in their mind. But you see I started going to church at the age of nineteen. So, my teachers in the ministry taught me and exposed me to the tricks of the enemy, and showed me how to warfare in the spirit realm. So, I had a very good start in becoming an adult. If you choose to be a loser instead of a winner, you will suffer greatly in life. Sometimes people go out on a limb too far and are never able to come back in, even if you through a rope out for them to grab hold, they have been out there so long until they lose hope in trying to get back in. This is a battle everybody has to fight, you have to choose whether you are going to fight and be a conqueror, are choose to stand there and be a loser thinking that you can't win the battle. You see this is where faith comes in, knowing that you are not in the battle alone, but God is in the battle with you

God never allows us to go to war with the devil by ourselves, he is there with us all the way, until we claim total victory, in every situation, that we get ourselves into with the devil. And with God on our side, in the ring with us we can't help but to come out a winner. I'm reminded when Jesus was on his way to carvery, he said these words, no man taketh my life, but I give my life for the sins of many. And after Jesus gave up the Ghost, he said it was finished. Went down to the pit of hell, preached to them that were already dead, and then gave them a chance to gain eternal life. Three days he was into the heart of the earth, and on that third day he rose just like he said he would. Beat Satan and take the key to eternal life. And when he got up out of the grave, he replied that all power has been given unto me, in heaven and earth. With God all things are possible. That's why you must choose ye this day whom you are going to serve. If you choose to live your life without God and instructions, then you choose to pay that price and be lost in the end. Because it is God who will lead you and guide you unto the knowledge of all truth and righteousness. No God no peace, Know God, Know peace. For there is a high price you pay for being disobedient. God will lead and guide you through life's journey. How can he lead you and guide you through your life journey if you choose not to serve him? There you do not know the path in which you are to take. You would be here and everywhere with no guide. But if you choose him, he will lead you and guide you in the path in which you are to take, so there for you cannot go wrong. I'm reminded of myself for at the age of seventeen I planned on leaving East, St. Louis, and moving to Chicago at the age of nineteen, knowing that it was not me but the Lord that was leading me and guiding me every step of the way. When I left East St. Louis at the age of nineteen, I got saved six months later. Therefore, it was not my intention to go to church to get saved at the age of nineteen. I had other plans to have a good time in the big city. So, therefore it was not I but God that was leading and guiding my footsteps. No man can walk a path that they know nothing about has never heard of or been taught. I thought twice about it, and if I wanted to walk that path or not. As I began to read the bible a fear came upon me, that I couldn't get rid of. So, therefore I stayed with the church. Therefore, it is very dangerous not to follow after God when he is leading and guiding you down a pathway of righteousness, and you choose not to go down the pathway he's trying to take you. As I began to grow in God, I saw how so many people who didn't have God, were in such bad condition, and their lives were in such a mess. As I looked around and saw people in that condition, I chose to stay with the Lord and continue down the highway of holiness. I started praying, and miracles started happening right away. Everything I prayed for started coming to me out of nowhere. For instance, I was at home on my knees crying and I was asking the Lore to give me a Job and not let me be homeless before I could get done praying, the telephone ranged, and it was human resources from Steward and Warner asking to speak to me, and ask if I am still interested in working for them, I said yes. Went in for an interview, and got the job. This was about the third miracle God had done for me from the time I left East, St. Louis. I can truly say that the Lord is a light unto my feet and a lamp unto my path. You cannot go wrong if you follow the light. And it will guide you down the path in which you should take. You cannot go wrong when you keep your eyes on the light, for Jesus is the light. But when you refuse instructions, and walk down the path you want to walk, for there are consequences you have to pay. Some of those consequences include being homeless, on alcohol, and drugs, mental illness, because you chose not to follow the right guide.

We all have to guide one on the right and one on the left. The guide that's on the right will lead you down the right path, where when you pray God will answer, meet every need, and also give you the desires of your heart.

And you have the guide on the left, that comes to steal, kill, and destroy. He leads you into a path of drugs and alcohol, causes you to be homeless, and has you living a life of drugs and crime. Sometimes when you get so far out there, there is a pathway of no return. And after going down the road of lies and crime, you already know where you are headed. And the end of that life of being disobedient is death.

But the end of the life of being obedient is having problems solved, and praying, allowing God to open doors and make ways for you as you serve him. We must stay on the pathway at all cost because our very life depends on it. Trouble befalls us all whether saved or unsaved, bond or free, we just have to have that faith in God that he is who he says he is, to the righteous, and the unrighteous. I haven't always been obedient, in all things. I have made many mistakes on this journey, sometimes doing things out of fear. I have served the Lord since age nineteen, and now I'm in my sixties, and I'm learning to pray first and most of all learning patience on how to wait upon the Lord. He that waited upon the Lord shall renew their strength, for they shall mount up as wings as eagles; they shall run and not be weary, they shall walk and not faint.

KJV 40:31

If you choose God this day, he will help you, and show you, how to walk in obedience. There are just so many people who live that's in shambles, and the majority of them Don't know how to come out and be free from the bondage that the devil put them in. That's our job, when the Lord saves you, God wants us to go forth, and show others how to break free and live a long healthy prosperous life. Jesus said whether they hear or fight against you, we are to tell them the truth if it costs us our lives.

Jesus said I wish that none should perish, but all would come unto repentance.

KJV 1ST Samuel 15:23

For rebellion is the sin of witchcraft; and stubbornness is as iniquity and Idolatry. Because though has rejected the word of the Lord, he hath rejected the from being King.

KJV 2nd Peter 3:9

CHAPTER-SEVEN

MARRIAGE AND BEING UNEQUALLY YOKED WITH UNBELIEVERS

I Was nineteen years old when I got saved, and I messed around and got married at the age of nineteen. I had to choose between getting married or leaving because of holiness. My religion doesn't allow me to live with a man and not be married. This was the guy I had met in Job - corps when I was sixteen years of age. So, I was warned to wait, but I went on anyhow and married the guy. It was bad, and I mean bad. I said I do and Lord help anybody that's save and marry someone outside of Christ. Earlier in chapter six, I explained to you the price you pay for being disobedient. I was disobedient, and didn't listen, and married the guy anyhow. The handwriting was on the wall just as plain as day. I married him out of fear of being alone in the city of Chicago. I was afraid and I was scared of not being able to take care of me. The marriage didn't lead to anything good.

Be ye not unequally yoked together with unbelievers. For what fellowship hath righteous with unrighteous? And what communion hath light with darkness. KJV 2nd Corinthians 6:14

If I had only listened and been obedient, I wouldn't had to go through what I went through. I got saved one Sunday morning and he got saved that same Sunday night, and we agreed to get married and continue. After we got married, he left the church. He got mixed up with the wrong people, using drugs, lying stealing cheating. But you see some of his behavior was already visible. I got a lawsuit settlement from a company I got hurt at, I hid the money at the house, I went to work the next day and he rambled until he found it, stole it and ram shacked the house, and pretended like someone else broke into the house4 and stole it. We got into a bad fight about it and I kept trying to leave the house and he wouldn't let me so we fought all night and he got hurt in the meantime. Two years into the marriage it got worse and worse, nothing changed. I kept going to church and in the meantime, I was getting stronger and stronger. He was out there, getting worse and worse. In and out of the mental hospital after overdosing and losing his mind. You see the devil doesn't care who he makes a fool out of. While you out there playing with God, the devil out there laughing at you. Because the devil knows that when God gets tired and fed up with you, he will turn you over, and the devil is going to have a field day with you. After being saved for about two years, I was called into the ministry. I answered the call, and I started street preaching, going around to the nursing homes and the hospitals, ministering, and laying hands on the sick. I started enjoying myself preaching and traveling. I realize marrying someone that's not in the Lord and not walking in the light as you are is a huge mistake, not only is it a huge but it is a dangerous mistake. I cannot count times that man kept running off with the dope man drugs, and almost got me killed numerous times. The dope man was at my house one Sunday when I got home from church, he attempted to approach me and I told him to back off of me, and I warned him to leave my house, and not come back because, I had nothing to do with the drugs he smoked up. I told him I was in the ministry, and I don't drink or smoke, and if you have a beef with him take it outside, and don't come back in my home again with that foolishness. He left and took him with him and whooped his tale until he went and got the money he smoked up. And now you understand how important it is to follow after God, and when he tells you no one. something, he already knows what lies ahead of you. And that is why it's important to be obedient and follow God's word. I had to continually fast and pray. It was times I had to leave my house and go and shut myself up in the church for three days and three nights fasting and praying, not knowing what shall befall me up ahead. I ran into many dangers with that man, but because I was in God, and I had people at the church fasting and praying for me, I was protected by the Holy Ghost, and God kept me. One thing about walking in the light, at least you can see where you are walking. Once you have made up your mind you are not going to be obedient to God, there are many hard lessons to learn especially being disobedient. You cannot see when you are walking in darkness, because you have no guide, and when you have no guide, you are on the wrong path, and when you are on the wrong path, you are going the wrong way. Down the road, you may see the sign the wrong way, hope and pray you turn around and start going in the other direction. The marriage I got myself into never got itself off the ground. I had a hard struggle for the first five years of the marriage, it didn't get better it got worse, and I was tired of crying until one day I decided to move on down the road, and keep it moving. At this point in life, it was time for me to throw in the towel on him. Because there were no changes, and he was not willing to change. I didn't know that he had been on drugs since he was fourteen years of age. He started taking his checks and buying drugs with his friend. His friend was more important than I. He wouldn't come home on Fridays, he would go with his friend and smoke all the money up except forty to fifty dollars, and then come home with that. That's why we shouldn't be unequally yoked together with unbelievers. They don't like the things you like, and you can't go to the places they go. When you are unsaved to are conformed to the things of this world, when God told us not to be conformed to the things of this world, but be ye transformed by the renewing of your mind. He wanted to hang out in the streets and party, and I went to church on Friday night. This is the reason why God wants us to be equally yoked. When you are equally yoked you can walk together and agree, but if you are unequally yoked, how can two walks together except they agree? I had to realize that time is moving on, and time waits on no man. I see that he has no plans of turning his life over to God. It was a high price I paid for trying to walk with someone who did not agree with me. And that is the price you have to pay or be unequally yoked with unbelievers. And it's the price you have to pay for being disobedient to the voice. When God tells you no, he means no. He will put all kinds of obstacles in your pathway to warn you not to go that road, and when you press over those obstacles and do it anyhow, there is a price to pay. After about five years, we kept going back and forth I saw that he didn't want anything in life, so it was time for me to go, and I left. He wanted the streets and I wanted nice cars, and a nice home, and he tried his best to stop me at everything I tried to do, every time I bought something he stole it and sold it. Who in the world wants to be married to someone like that? Not only did he steal all the material things out of the house he stole all the food out of the freezer, the kid's video games, and their clothes too. And he took my clothes and sold them. That was the price I had to pay for not listening to God and pressing over the blocks he had put in my way, to let me know not to marry him. But you see I only made one mistake, I did not make the same mistake twice, and I did not. I was just so miserable with that man I left town and left him on the streets because I couldn't take that anymore. I realized after he had robbed my church bank account it was time to go. Do you see what the devil was trying to do, he was trying to get me to kill him. So, I refused to allow the devil to make me kill him, so I left and put it in God's hand and let him take care of it because one of God's commandments is that thou shalt not kill, and I refuse to let the devil make a fool out of me, and allow my anger to get in the way and do something I will regret for the rest of my life. There is an old saying, No God, No Peace, Know God, Know Peace, that is a true saying. When you don't have God, you don't have no peace. Our peace is in the Lord because we can call on him when we get into trouble. Sometimes we don't have to get into trouble, because trouble can find you anywhere. I cried for so many years until I kept asking God how much longer I had to go through this until finally I just gave up and walked away. And every time I prayed about that man, I heard the voice of God speak to me and say I am alpha and the omega; the beginning and the ending; saith the Lord, which is, and which was, and which is to come the Almighty.

KJV: Revelations 8:1

When God had spoken that to me, I understood exactly what he was saying. He was letting me know that when everything is all said and done, he will have the last say in the conclusion of the matter.

Is anything too difficult or too wonderful for the Lord? At the appointed time; when the season for her delivery comes, I will return to you, and Sarah will have a son. KJV Genesis 18:14

I had to step out on faith and continue on the journey that I started. I was a little afraid and scared, but God showed me that he would be with me until the end. It's been forty-one years now, and God has not given me another husband to help me he let me know that he is going to take care of me unto the end and he has done just that. When I had to go through the fire God was with me, so that I wouldn't be burned. When I went through the waters, it did not overtake me, and when I went through the flood, I did not drown. His word is powerful, and sharper than any two-edged sword.

One thing that I do know is that the foundation of God stands a sure. Not one jot or one word of God will fall to the ground; when he sends his word out, it will accomplish, what he sent it out to do. Our hope all not to be built on nothing less; than Jesus Christ and his righteousness. For I say to you that the foundation of God stands sure. I'm the type of person I do not like to carry unnecessary burdens, because it's enough to be able to go through your trials in your everyday life, instead of doing things that you know that it's not becoming Holiness and causing more trouble to come upon yourself. Always Let God Be God.

Listen to People: Be Ye Not Unequally Yoked with Unbelievers.

CHAPTER EIGHT

———

RAISING CHILDREN AS A SINGLE MOTHER

Unto the woman he said, I will Greatly multiply thy sorrow and thy conception; in sorrow thy shalt bring Forth children; and thy desire shalt be to thy husband, and he shall rule over thee.

KJVGenesis 3:16

As you know earlier in the first chapter I stated how I was from a family of thirteen children, being raised by a single mother, when the father tried to kill my mother when we were just small children. He cut my mother up 898 stitches and then took off and ran, leaving her for dead, and didn't even think about the children. We never saw him again until the majority of us were grown and left home. I was about twenty when I saw and heard from him. He decided to come back to East St. Louis with no apologies, no nothing he sent us some money before he came back. Even his own family was upset with him for what he had done. According to the law he was supposed to be charged with attempted manslaughter. Not only did he try to kill her, but he was going to kill everybody in the house that night. I and my oldest brother busted out the door and ran around and around the neighborhood that night. I grew up and moved to Chicago. I was in my early twenties when one of my sisters, had a son and didn't want him. So, I offered to take him, me, and my ex-husband. She got scared and didn't give him up right away, so a few months later, children's services stepped in, because she didn't want to feed him or change his diaper. So, one of my sisters brought him to Chicago and I ended up taking him. When she asked me to take him, I replied you don't want him I'll take him. And so, it was. She gave him to my mother, and my mother said she couldn't raise anymore, and that she was tired because she still had four children of her own to raise. So, I agreed to take him. And a few years later my younger sister had a little girl, that she didn't want to, I agreed to take her, so now I have two different sisters' kids in my possession. And then I adopted two more children from Columbus Ohio. I was in the ministry at that time. After the last two that came out of Columbus Ohio, I decided not to take anymore.

By this time, I had become single, when I decided to take on these four children. I didn't think that the responsibility was going to be so difficult, Trying to raise all four of them by myself. It wouldn't have been so hard if there hadn't been one of them while manipulating the other three. If I had got rid of the oldest one, I think the other three would have been all right. But the oldest one which is my nephew lied and deceived all three of them. He was so manipulative until he destroyed the whole plan that I had put together. I would leave and give them chores to do before I got back, and he would tell them that they didn't have to do it because I wasn't nobody's mother. And when I got back home the chores weren't done, so they found themselves in a world of trouble. One thing I wrote in another chapter is where there is no love there is no respect. He was angry about him not being with his real mother. So, he acted a fool until he was seventeen, and then I showed him the door. Started getting high, coming into the house at three and four o'clock in the morning, thinking I was just a pushover. I had to show him that he couldn't live up in here and do what he wanted to do, whenever he gets ready to do it. You know that he was a young black scholar. He had received black scholar awards, carrying a GPA of 4.0. Got a letter of recommendation from President Bill Clinton; to go wherever he wanted to go or do in the world. Well, he let the devil make a fool out of him and through a scholarship away that Opera Winfrey had given him. He would have had his education paid for from the seventh grade to the twelfth grade. He went in to take the SSAT test and deliberately failed it. So, when he failed the test, the private school we had chosen for him to go to rejected him. I called and asked what was the hold-up, and they told me that they were not going to accept him because his test scores weren't adding up with his GPA. I knew then he was playing games with adults. And I was not going to stand for that foolishness in my house. So, when he was seventeen, I showed him the door, and I never looked back. Believe me, right about now he is paying for it, and he has not paid for it like he's going to. This is another reason why I'm writing this book about life on the streets without God and education. There is a great price you have to pay when you don't have respect for your elders, and you think that you know everything, as to where no one can tell you anything because you are so disrespectful to teachers, mother, and were very disrespectful to military high officials. He threw his life away, and when he got done acting out, he lost out in the end. This is the reason he was teaching the other three to do the same thing. The other three followed in his footsteps. They all walked out of the house behind him and I left one in Dayton Ohio, back in foster care, and the other two pulled the same stump, and I left them in foster care in Indianapolis, IND. So, the two I adopted are doing well, but the niece and the oldest nephew are not doing well at all. The niece walked out at sixteen, saying she was not going to summer school, so that she could make up some of her credit hours, so she left. And I left her right there. She now has five children by different men with no high school diploma and no job. She states she is a stay-at-home mom. I warned them every day that they resided in my home, and what would happen if they didn't go to school and get an education. She's on welfare food stamps and section eight housing. Know you see the penalty for not having respect for adults. It was hard raising other people's children. They had no love and no respect for my home. So, I had to keep it moving. I would tell anybody how hard it is being a single mother especially when you are trying to raise other people's children. We had s system going, but you will always have one in the bunch that is going to be defiant. The only thing they had to do was to keep their living quarters clean and everybody cleaned up after themselves. I had to go to work and try to put them through school by myself. I had some help when my mother came to live with me, she was the babysitter. And she kept watch on them while I went to work. And I had a stressful job. I drove a bus for thirty-one years, and it was so stressful dealing with the public. So, my mom was a great blessing for me, because I didn't have to worry about a babysitter. I was living in Dayton, Ohio at the time, driving the bus for the city of Dayton, Ohio. Me and my mom cooked on the weekends so that the kids would have a hot meal when they came home from school. And if they didn't want leftovers, they had the option to heat dinners that were in the freezer, fix sandwiches, or whatever they wanted, as long as they cleaned up after themselves. So, I couldn't figure out what is the problem. They had bikes, games, and skates and could go outside whenever they wanted to. These children were adopted, and they had the worst attitude someone could ever have. Plus, they were the most ungrateful kids I had ever had to deal with. I was young at that time, and good thing I was, because no older person could ever be able to go through that. I thank God I had a little experience in helping raise children. Because my mother had thirteen children, and we had to help her out with the younger children when they came home after school. For instance, cook clean and make sure they have a bath before going to bed. And we had to comb the girl's hair, and I learned how to cut the boy's hair. When I adopted the four, I already knew how to cut the boy's hair and I kept braids on the girl's hair. I didn't think adopting the four would be a great problem because we had to take care of at least eight of them at my mom's house.

At my mom's house, we had to cook for fourteen people, including my mother. She went to school in the daytime and had a part-time job at night, to help keep the family going. I do appreciate my mother because she was all that we had. She tried and she did her best. I never heard her complain, or regret that she had all of us until everybody was grown. That's because when some of them got grown they began to talk back curse her out and one or two of them even attempted to put their hands on her. So, when we were at home helping out, we started teaching the children how to fold their laundry and showed them how to put it away and make their beds before they left in the morning for school.

When I started teaching the four children, I adopted the same method, beds had to be made before leaving for school. And then as they got older, I started teaching them how to vacuum after meals and showed them how to rinse the dishes and put them into the dishwasher. I was trying to teach them early so that they would know how to take care of their children when they grow up and have their own family. Raising those four children with the bad attitudes they had made me so depressed. I refuse to let them see me being depressed. You see when you are serving God, he knows just how to bring you out of a situation that's got you down. It is so important to have family or friends to be able to help out when you need a break. Because you are going to need one. I was fortunate to get a brake because my mom moved in to help me out. So, I was able to go to work without worrying about what was going on at the house because the four children I had were so sneaky, that they just couldn't be trusted at all. My mom helped out with the cooking and the laundry and with the supervising of the children. My mother would see to them getting their homework done and getting their bath before bedtime. It was two of them that gave me the most problems my nephew, and my niece. My niece didn't want to do anything she just didn't want to take care of herself, she fought every day, and she didn't want to go to school, she fought about that.

I was so glad when she reached the age of sixteen, she walked out of the house and put herself in the system, and the system didn't put up with her at all. In about six months they had her emancipated and got her apartment, and she could not even do that. She was on the streets for a minute. Then she started having all those children. I wonder how can you take care of five children and cannot take care of yourself. She was expecting one of the other children to help her out, but she got fooled, and she was warned about everything she had got herself into. She thought I was lying to her and knew she was getting ready to find out about life all by herself. Wait until the children go into adolescence, she is going to get a surprise because some of them are going to do the same things she did, and then maybe she will see herself. I didn't have any children of my own because I was married to a man who had been on drugs and alcohol ever since he was fourteen years of age. So that was the reason I chose not to have any because I didn't want to see those poor children come out like him. It wouldn't have been fair to me or fair to the children.

When I decided to take on the responsibility of those four children, my priority was to make sure those children were well provided for, such as a nice clean house, utility food clothes, and shelter, clean uniforms, and make sure school fees were paid, and the only thing they had to do is go to school and get an education. Even though I was working long hours, I still had my mother there supervising them in the way that they were supposed to go. And another thing is I kept them in the church, so they don't have an excuse when they get grown, and go in a way that they shouldn't go in, you went that way because you refuse to learn obedience and respect for your elders. That is a lesson you will learn once your mind is set in that direction. You want to tell everybody else what to do but you don't want nobody telling you what to do because you think that you know it all. Nobody knows it all, when you put yourself into that situation, where you know everything, you have just stopped growing. As long as we are alive in life, no matter how old we get, we still should be able to learn.

Now you see how hard it is in life to try to raise children as a single mother. You will get burnt out so quickly. This is why a lot of people end up not keeping the children, putting them into foster care, start using drugs and alcohol, and even giving the children to other family members to take care of them. Because it is very hard trying to raise children as a single mother. If you know like I know, I wouldn't want anybody having children without a husband and trying to raise them kids all by themselves. As I am still in the ministry until this very day, and I still encourage young people in the church to wait until they get married first, before they start having children.

CHAPTER-NINE

FOR I HAVE PAID MY DUES In My Youth

As Jesus was teaching, he replied that I must work the work of him that sent me while it is day the night cometh when no man will be able to work. The word of God tells us to remember now thy creator in the days of our youth, while the evil days come not, nor the years draw nigh, when thou shall say, I have no pleasure in them.

ECCLESIATES 12: I

While the sun, or the light, or the moon, or the stars, be not darkened, nor the clouds return after the rain.

ECCLEIATES 12: 2

While you are young and strong, we need to consider working for the Lord. While we have our health and strength, and able to go and be able to perform the work of the Lord, while we are yet young and tender. God can use us when we are not sick and feeble. I was only nineteen years of age when I came to God. I saw signs and wonders being performed at a young age. And by seeing signs and wonders, that brought me unto the belief that I have today. And that was forty-three years ago. I have traveled from the North to the South. And from the East to the West working the works of the Lord. For I have paid my dues in my youth. The first half of my journey is over. I have been in the Evangelist field for forty-three years and know the time has come for me to build a Church from the ground up and start my Pastoral Ministry. I started noticeably young, and to this day I have no regrets, about giving the Lord my Life at the age of fourteen. I am so grateful to God that he chose me at an early age. Many people do not get that opportunity to give their life to God that early. Many others can give their life over to God at an early age, but they do not. And then some lived to get old and began to think about what they should have done when God called them in their youth. Be not deceived my brother for many are called, but very few are chosen. I am so glad that when God called me at the age of nineteen, I humbled myself dropped everything, and went and followed Jesus. God put me into the Holiness Church of God, where there was nothing but older people there. I was the youngest one in the Church saved. I sat under the elders for my teaching. Everything was not perfect nor were the people perfect. But I took what I could get, and I ran with it. They showed me how to go out on the street corners to minister to lost souls. On my days off, this is what I and a few others had done. Remember what Jesus said, I must work the work of him that sent me while it is day, the night comes when no man would be able to work. Believe me, my dear brethren nighttime will come into your life, whether you are saved or not. Trials and tribulations will arise when you least expect them to. I started college, to go back to school and get my GED and to get a degree. After I enrolled in college, I studied for my GED, and I started a major in Computer Science. Therefore, I enrolled in Malcolm X College to get a head start on education. They had a Christian Ministry on the campus, so I joined, and in our spare time, we all got together and had bible class on the campus. We would go into some of the empty classrooms and have our daily prayer. However, that did not last too long, because when we started praying the other classrooms would hear us and chase us out. So, we decided to go to the auditorium to have prayer, however, that did not work either, the entire school heard us praying, and they chased us out of there too. I remember going into a classroom one day to pray, and the other students who were with us needed to be filled with the Holy Ghost. So, I ask them a question, how are you all waiting to be filled? They answered and said we are just standing here waiting. So, I showed them what they must do while they are waiting, you must tarry while you are waiting, so they asked me how we do that, I replied that you must start by thanking Jesus, so here we go we all started saying thank you Jesus, and after a short while the power of the Holy Ghost fell, and those that were seeking got filled that very same hour. Ad I got healed that very same day. It was so amazing to see the power of God fall on those who were seeking to be filled with God's power. And the entire school heard us, and they came again and chased us out of the classroom once again. I saw miracle after miracle in my youth, that led me to believe there was a God somewhere. As I was riding the CTA bus back in the late seventies, I was looking out the window up into the clouds, and the clouds were so pretty and white, and the sky was so blue. And then I ask the Lord a question. I ask him to do anyone else see the sky and the clouds as I see them. I saw the clouds with power in them and the sky was so pretty and blue. And someone was sitting about two seats behind me, and I heard them say look at those clouds, they have so much power in them. And they said look at the sky, it is so pretty and blue, it looks like something you have never seen before. I turned around and looked at the person who was sitting two rows behind me. And I ask the Lord that man answered my question I had addressed you with. I never opened my mouth and spoke out. That led me to believe that God knew every thought we were thinking. He answered my question through another human being who was sitting on the bus. So, the church started teaching me how to pray, and I started learning how to lay a hand on the sick. I have seen many people healed in my young life until it led me to have the belief that I have on today. I had a little sister who had got hold of some Drano when she was two years of age. She went through surgery after surgery. She stayed in the hospital for a long time. After she drank out of a glass that had Drano in it, it ate up her esophagus and it ate up one of her legs until one ended up being longer than the other one. She had to wear a tracheid in her throat to help her breathe. They had to make her special shoes to wear to try and build her legs back up.

She ended up having surgery after surgery. They took some of the intestines to rebuild her esophagus back up. She had to eat out of a feeding tube until she was able to be able to eat through her mouth again. This situation was so painful for our family until my mom let me go up to the hospital at times to stay with her and keep her company. The people at the hospital allowed me to stay there with her, and they would feed me along with her. When she did finally come home, my mother showed me how to change her trach, and I learned how to clean it. After all that, my father ran off and cut my mother up nine hundred and ninety-eight stitches, and then he left all thirteen of us. We had to help mom cook, clean, and make sure the little ones got fed and got their bath. I was the one that took care of my little sister. When she started school, I would have my lunch at school, because we were able to get free lunches, then I would leave school, and come home and get her and take her back to school because she had started kindergarten. Then I would pick her up at the end of the school day and bring her back home. This was the most crucial time in our life for a sister to drink some Drano, and a father who cuts our mother up and leaves her for dead, not knowing what tomorrow holds for our family. After I was grown, I sat down and cried so many nights, thinking about the life we had to go through and the pain and suffering we had to endure. Because of what I and my other twelve siblings had to endure, made me a more compassionate person, as where I would see others in need and would always lend to them that are without. Even as I am writing this story, I am in so many tears, knowing that somebody like me made it through a struggle like that and then survived to be able to write about this story. Through the hard times and the difficult situations, we were put in we survived. This situation that we grew up in led me to write this book, that is called Life on the Streets without God and Education. Knowing this a father who runs off and leaves behind thirteen children, and almost kills the mother, did not have any love and respect for anyone. But we all made it to be an adult. Eleven finished high school or with a GED and two refused to go. Not bad growing up with a single mother and no dad, with thirteen children. And I want everybody to know that my sister who got hold of Drano finished high school. She even moved to Chicago with me and started college at Malcolm X just as I did. She did not finish but she tried. She lived until she was twenty-nine years of age. Just days before her thirtieth birthday she passed away with a Grand Mile seizure. I remember when I got saved in the late seventies, I went home and my sister the age of fifteen still had the trach in her throat, and the specially made shoes on, so I called her off to the side and asked her to let me pray for her. I prayed that the Lord would remove the trach and grow her legs back to the same size, and he did just that. The same year she went in for a doctor visit, and they removed the trach and allowed the hole to close, so therefore she was able to breathe on her own. Before she graduated from high school both of her legs were back at the same size, and she no longer needed the specially made shoes. Oh, what a mighty God we serve. Nobody can do this type of miracle but God. Therefore, we must work the works of him that sent us while it is day because when night comes no man would be able to work. Serve God while you are young because God can use you freely when you are not able to think on your own. As you get older your mind is set in your way, in which while you are young you have not grown into your own will yet. When you are young you do not know as much, as if you were older. When I got saved, I only knew what God was leading me to do. I did what I was instructed to do no more or no less. I had to learn how to follow God's orders. Sometimes it is not an easy thing to do, because you must learn how to distinguish between the two voices. Sometimes God would tell you to do some things and the other voice would tell you not to do it. For I want you to know that I have paid my dues in my youth. The forty-three years of traveling and raising four adopted kids, while traveling over the country, was not an easy task. And putting up with a husband who was on drugs, stealing everything he could steal from the house and the kids. Including food and clothes. So, as I thought along the way, Lord I am tired, something must give.

So, I would not give the kids up because they needed me, so I decided to run off and leave him on the street corner. Right where he should have been left. When I got myself out of that situation, I made a promise never to get back into a situation again where there is drugs and alcohol are involved in a person's life. My advice to you is that you serve the Lord while you are young and have your health and strength. You never know what will happen to you down the road. You never know when a tragedy will strike you are your family. I have no regrets about serving God in my youth. I have had so many miracles be performed before my eyes in my youth, until if I decide to tell it all, one or two books cannot contain all. I had made a decree with myself to never have any children with a man on drugs or a man who does not want to work. I have held to my standard until this day. I am sixty-two years of age and I stood by my word. I am more determined than ever before to finish the course that the Lord our God has laid before me.

I remember getting saved at the age of nineteen and being called to the Ministry at the age of twenty-one. At the age of twenty-three, I was called to leave Chicago, Illinois, and go to Dallas, Texas. This was the first state I started in the Evangelist field. Before I left Chicago, I was there for five years, before I left and went into Dallas, Texas. I walked to church or rode the bus for five years, and I never missed a Sunday or any type of service that was being held at my church. I was faithful for five years to God, and here I yet remain faithful until right to this day, forty-three years later. On my way out of the city of Chicago, I received a word of Prophecy from our Pastor Elsie Brown, and she told me that the Lord said from this day on I shall never walk again. Not many days from that day when the Word of God went forth, the Lord blessed me with a Lincoln, a Mark-five. And as I began my journey into Dallas Texas, I drove off the lot with the Mark Five. And I headed on down the road and went in and got set up. I was there for about two years, and I had taken on my little nephew and brought him along with me. He was not in school yet, he was only three. I headed out on my way to San Francisco and stayed there for about one year. Then I headed out to Boston Massachusetts, and I was there for about four years. Then I went back to Dallas, Texas for about another three years. Then moved to Dayton, Ohio, where I took my sister's daughter, and I adopted a sister and a brother out of Columbus Ohio. From Dayton Ohio to Indianapolis, Indiana. From Indiana to Tampa Bay Florida. While I was in Dallas Texas, I learned how to drive the school. They trained me for my CDLs, and I stayed with the school bus for a year, and then I went and applied for a bus driving job at the transit authority at Dallas Area Rapid Transit Authority. And now not only have experience in computers, but I also have experience in driving a bus. So, now wherever I went I had a job that only required having a CDL, and I possessed one too. Everywhere I went, I could get a good-paying job right away. After leaving Tampa Bay Florida, the Lord spoke to me and said I must go back home, which was my hometown East St. Louis Illinois. I did not want to go back there, but I had no other choice. So, I packed up and went back to East St. Louis, and after being there for about a year, my mother passed away, and that was about the saddest day of my life. Because about twenty of those years, me and my mother lived together and traveled the country together. She was my babysitter while I went to work. I have never paid for childcare. You must remember knowing thy creator in the days of thy youth. I no longer had the kids they had all left, so I was free to do whatever the Lord wanted me to do. I was there in St. Louis for about ten years, and the Lord transitioned me to Chicago. Now I started a new job, driving the Mega Bus. I get a chance to meet people from all walks of life. And I was able to Minister to them and pray for people all over the World. It was a stressful job but God was able to bring me through it and bring me out of it. Ministry is awfully hard, it is not an easy task, because you must deal with so many personalities, and you must pray for the wisdom to know how to deal with every person. It is like people with more than one child. You must find the wisdom to deal with each child in its own way because no two children are alike. Every child has its character, and it must be dealt with separately. Just like God deals with every Christian in its way. No two Christians are alike, neither is our calling of God alike. It might be similar, but it is not the same. God calls us at different ages, some young, some old, some middle age, but God has called us all unto Holiness, and that calling is the same for every man, woman, boy, and girl. But you know that the calling in the gifts operates the same. Even unto the fivefold Ministry. Every person is given a gift, a role, and a part to play in the body of Christ for us to continue the work that Christ had started while he was down here on this earth. Whether you are young, old, or middle age you have a job to do in the body of Christ. Just as you wake up every day to go on man's job, you ought to be faithful working for God, and give God the same obedience on his job as you do on man's job. For I was young when I got started working for God, and I do not regret one day of serving the Lord, because it is rewarding and joyful. I have had great joy in teaching and preaching the word of the Lord for over forty years. My greatest peace has been in Ministry. For I have paid my dues in my youth. For I have completed one half of my journey, and now at the age of sixty-two the second half of my journey begins. Started in Ministry at the age of twenty-one, and at the age of twenty-three went on the Evangelist field until the age of sixty, now going into Pastoral until the closing of my journey. Ts been a long journey, and hard journey, but it has been a rewarding journal. Not only the natural but also physical and spiritual blessings have taken place for me down through the years. You must be willing and obedient to work for the Lord, when he calls you must answer. I came out of East St. Louis Illinois, to Chicago Illinois, from Chicago Illinois to Dallas Texas, from Dallas Texas to San Francisco California, Boston Massachusetts, from Boston Mass to, Trotwood Ohio, from Trotwood Ohio to, Indianapolis Indiana to, Tampa Bay Florida, from Tampa Bay Florida to, East St. Louis Illinois, from East St. Louis Illinois back to Chicago Illinois for retirement. Sometimes along the journey, I got tired, and sometimes disappointment set in, but God has always been there to carry me. I have been misunderstood, but God was there, when lied to and talked about, God has been there. For I want you to know that I sacrificed everything to be able to carry the Ministry of Christ to the four corners of the world. And I have not completed the full course of my journey that God has assigned unto me. This year 2021 starts a new chapter of the second half of the journey God has entrusted unto me. And I am determined to complete the Ministry God has laid before me and to carry out every instruction that the spirit of the Lord gives me. Even though sometimes it is hard because the enemy will have you believe you cannot, and then the enemy will have you too scared to open your mouth and tell what thus said by the Lord. I have been obedient many times and told different individuals would fight against me after I spoke what this said to the Lord. when the Lord speaks, I must tell them what thus said the Lord. And most of them had come out against me and started persecuting me against what I had spoken to them according to the word of the Lord. Nevertheless, God was right there with me, to bring me through it. If he bought me to it, he would bring me through it. You must be willing to give up the things you love the most, to be able to walk with the Lord and to be able to be in his presence. For I have paid my dues in my youth although it has not been an easy journey. It has been a long journey and a hard journey. From the start of Chicago to Dallas Texas was the easy part, after Dallas the journey has been getting harder and harder. Even after the adoption taking care of four children, was the most difficult task I have ever encountered. The most difficult part is dealing with four different personalities. In which you have one bad apple in the bunch that ends up ruining the whole group. You can preach and teach all you want, but it takes an individual to want to change their ways. And until this very day the one that had the bad attitude still has not changed his ways nor has, he made any improvements to the way he treats people right till this day and it has been thirty-six years ago. And it is sad to say that the other three children have adopted the same old mean attitude in how they treat God and other people. I never thought that in many years I would raise children as to where they would denounce God. It was a terrible situation when I read the comments on social media, concerning one of the children, talking about we taught her about a false God that did not exist. Not only was it disturbing, but it was also depressing to hear such a comment that was made concerning her teaching. It has caused her to live a life that she was not taught to live. Not only is she living badly with five children and no husband, but she is also in poverty in and out of the different food banks and living on section eight where she does not have to pay any rent, and she still cannot get herself together to be able to give these children the life that they deserve. She was raised by me from, the age of one-year-old, where Her mother was one of my youngest sisters, who passed away when my niece was five years of age. She has been taught of God and she was warned about what would happen if she did not go to school and get an education. She walked out of the house and turned herself over to the state of Indiana. She declared that she was not going to go to summer school to catch up on her credits so that she could graduate on schedule, and that was the action that she took. And now she must pay a high price for not going to school and getting an education. This is one of the reasons I chose to write this book Life on The Streets Without God and Education. There is an extremely high price you must pay if you do not go to school and get an education. And not having God in this day and time is streamlining dangerous. Because there is an old saying that goes no God no peace. Know God know peace. For there is no peace to the wicked said the Lord. How can you have good luck on your side when you do not listen to anybody? Everybody is wrong but you. When you have your own opinion and what others tell you does not matter because you are right about it, and everybody else is wrong in your opinion. It is a hard task for God to do something with you when your mind is already set to go in the direction you want to go in. There is no reason in life to argue with a person who is in that state of mind because you cannot convince them that the sky is blue, they will always see the sky as the color that they say it is. Forty-three years in Holiness and one thing that I have learned is that there is a reality in serving a true and living God. Too many miracles have been performed right before my eyes. Doors have been opened that were shut, and ways have been made from no way. I have seen men and women turn their lives over to God. You cannot convince me we do not have a higher power up above controlling things down here on this earth. For if you believe you will receive. If you deny God, you will be denied the blessings that are down here on this earth. The struggle for you is going to be real. And there is no getting around it, either you will acknowledge God and be blessed of him or you will denounce him and be cursed of him. For this one thing that I am sure of, there is a reality in serving a true and living God. There must be some type of hope in every living human being, for if there are none bad things are surely to happen. Each one of us must have some type of hope in something or someone. For I have paid my dues in my youth, traveling to and from throughout the country. Convincing men and women everywhere that Christ Jesus lives. And yet my journey is not complete, because I have a second half to complete before the end of my days has expired. God did not create us to be in the world to lurk around and do nothing. For we all have a calling in our life, whether we answer it or not the calling will never depart. If you leave this world and do not answer the call, there will be a hard penalty you have to pay for not answering your call. It does not make any sense to me to just be here in the world doing nothing with your life and then have the nerve to get mad at the ones that are trying. We who are trying to fulfill God's will make mistakes, but we learn from them, and we keep pushing to complete the mission that God has set before us. I started my journey at the age of nineteen, and I am sixty-two years of age now, and I am not tired yet. I am still pressing toward the mark of a higher calling of God that is in Christ Jesus. Whether young or old or middle age I hope this book encourages you to look unto God which is the beginning and the end of all things. And that you find your place in God and labor in your calling just as I did. I got so much joy and peace out of preaching and praying for people until it encouraged me to keep on doing it. And the more you do it the greater the anointing of God comes upon you. And there is no greater feeling than being in the presence of the Lord. Once you start you will never turn back to the world, because the world has nothing to offer you. For there is hope in the Lord, there is education in the Lord, there is promotions in the Lord. What you need or looking for is in the name of the Lord. For there is also prosperity in the Lord, and peace, love, and joy, and happiness in him.

I hope that my story will help you to become a writer and be able to tell your story. Your story is important also. Everybody has a story to tell, and by reading my story, I hope that it will help you find your way and that you will gain the strength to overcome every obstacle that stands in your way, so that you may be able to get the job done and be able to find your place in God and be able to complete your assignment that the Lord has assigned you to. And to enjoy the benefits of the Lord in which he has in store for you. Whether it be in the natural or the spirit realm. And to be able to seek education that is out there for you to be able to live a long productive life in Christ Jesus. For the Lord is a provider and a way maker for all that seek him and call upon his name. He will never leave you nor will he forsake those that put their trust in him.

24. And the servant of the Lord must not strive; but be gentle unto all men, apt to teach, patient.

25. In meekness instructing those that oppose themselves if God peradventure will give them repentance to the acknowledging of the truth.

26. And that they may recover themselves out of the snare of the devil, who are taken captive by him at his will.

11 TIMOTHY 2: 24-26

For if I labor for the Lord day and night
God will give me the strength to finish this fight.
The race is not to the swift
Neither the battle given to the strong
But given to him that endures unto the end.

CHAPTER-TEN

TO KNOW GOD IS TO LOVE GOD

PSALMS 34: 8

O taste and see that the Lord is good; blessed is the man that trusted in him.

PSALMS 34: 9

O fear the Lord ye his saints: For there is no want to them that fear him.

In my forty-three years in Holiness, I find that to know God is to love God. As I began to search, and seek to find out who God is, he is someone you cannot help but to love. God wants us to love him with our whole heart soul and mind. One of the commandments states that we must love the Lord thy God with our whole heart soul and mind. And that we shall have no other God before him. For the Lord, our God is a jealous God. It took me a while to figure out who and what I was getting ready to serve in my young days. I found out that God would be just what you would let him be to you. I tried him as a burden barrier. He was to me a wheel in the middle of a wheel. He was my way out of many trials and tribulations that I had to go through. When I was in trouble, he delivered me from of all my troubles. He has been my bread when I was hungry. He put food on my table when I did not have food. I tried him as a bill payer. God will be just what you let him be to you. To know God is to love God.

PSALMS 146: 3

For God has warned us not to put our trust in princes, nor in the son of man, in whom there is no help. You must make the decision on your own to come into the knowledge of knowing who God is to you. For our God is many different things to many people. For everyone see God different to who and what he is to them. For our God is a spirit and they that worship him must worship him in spirit and in truth. I have been saved for forty-three years, and I have seen many miracles done before my eyes, even through prayers, I had been praying as a child. I started having vision and dreams as a child. Every night when I went to bed, there was a fear on me because I kept seeing in my room that was full of fog. And I did not understand it, because during the fog, I could not see anything, so I hid under the covers scared to death. And I kept having the same dreams over and over. And in those dreams was a bear kept trying to get me, I ended up escaping every time. And then I had dreams about a werewolf kept chasing me, but I escaped every time. Then there was the dream about a vampire after me I got away every time. Then after I got grown and moved to Chicago the bad dreams stopped. I noticed that my years of being saved at the age of nineteen, people have tried their best to come against me and hurt me. But God has been my shield and my buckler. He has been my protector, and he has sent his angels to keep charge over me because of the calling that is upon my life. The devil set out to destroy my life at an early age, but it was not so. Because under the shadow of the almighty, I had put my trust. To know God is to love God. When I arrived in Chicago at the age of nineteen, things were hard because I got connected with people that did not want the same things as I did. So, after I got saved, I had to separate myself from those people, and follow God. And after carefully viewing my decision, I found out later down the road, I had made the right decision for my own life. You must be strong enough and mature enough to be able to make the right decisions for your life. For one thing that I have found out that there is no failure in God. If there is any failure or fault it lies within us. For at the age of nineteen, God has bought me. For if it had not been for the Lord, I would not know where I would be unto this day.

PSALMS 30: 5

For his anger endures but a moment; in his favor is life: Weeping may endure for a night, but joy comes in the morning. Things will get hard sometimes on this highway of holiness, but know this one thing that stands assure, that God will be there every step of the way. Sometimes it feels like he has turned his back on you, but he told us in his word that he hid his face from us for a season, he wants to make sure no matter what you go through are you still going to trust him to the end. But then when he told us in his word that he hid his face from us for a season, he said that with everlasting kindness will he gather us. To know God is to love God. The more you seek to know who God the more wonderful things you will find out about him, and that makes you fall in love with him even more. I reminded of Saul as he was on his way down to Damascus.

ACTS 22: 1-9 KJV

Mean while Saul, still breathing threats and murder against the disciples of the Lord, went to the high priest and ask him for letters to the synagogues at Damascus, so that if he found any who belonged to the way, men, or women, he might bring them bound to Jerusalem.

As he neared Damascus on his journey, suddenly a light from heaven flashed around him. He fell to the ground and heard a voice say to him, Saul, Saul, why do you persecute me? Who are you, Lord? Saul asked. I am Jesus, whom you are persecuting, he replied. You see Saul knew who the Lord was all the time, because he asks the Lord who was he. This was the start of the transformation of Saul, and after he had been transformed God change his name to Paul. And Jesus said unto Saul it is hard for them to kick against the prick. And he trembling and astonished said, Lord what will thou have me to do? And the Lord said unto him, arise, and go into the city, and it shall have told thee what thou must do. And the men who journeyed with him stood speechless, hearing a voice, but seeing no man. And Saul arose from the earth; and when his eyes were opened, he saw no man. In other words, God had blinded Saul. But they led him by the hands and bought him into Damascus. And he was three days without sight, neither did he eat nor drink.

ACTS 22: 10-19 KJV

And there was a certain disciple at Damascus, named Ananias; and to him saith the Lord in a vision, Ananias. And he said, behold I am here, Lord. And the Lord said unto him, arise go into the street, which is called straight, and inquire in the house of Judas for one called Saul, of Tarsus: for, behold, he prays, and hath seen in a vision a man named Ananias coming in, and putting his hand on him, that he might receive his sight. Then Ananias answered, Lord, I have heard by many of this man, how much evil he has done to the saints at Jerusalem: And here he has authority from the chief priest to bind all that call on thy name. But the Lord said unto him, go thy way for he is a chosen vessel unto me, to bear my name before the gentiles, and kings, and the children of Israel. For I will show him how great things he must suffer for my name's sake. And Ananias went his way, and entered the house, and putting his hands on him said Brother Saul, the Lord even Jesus, that appeared unto the in the way as they came, hath sent me, that thou might receive thy sight, and be filled with the Holy Ghost. And immediately there fell from his eyes as it had been scales: and he received sight for with, and arose, and was baptized. And when he had received meat, he was strengthened. Then was Saul certain days with the disciples which were at Damascus.

For know do you see that it is hard to come into contact wit the Lord Jesus Christ and not be converted. For to know God, is to love God. I have experience miracle after miracle during these forty-three years I have been in Holiness. And it has been so amazing to pray for everything you need and the things you desire come to pass right before your eyes. Who would not put their trust in a God like him? I tried him, and I found him to be faithful, and true.

PSALMS 27:1-14 KJV

For I am reminded of David in the twenty-seven Psalms when he said that the Lord is my light and my salvation, whom shall, I fear? The Lord is the strength of my life; of whom shall I be afraid?

When the wicked, even mine enemies and my foes, came upon me to eat up my flesh, they stumbled and fell.

Though a host should encamp against me, in this will I be confident.

One thing have I desired of the Lord, that will I seek after; that I may dwell in the house of the Lord all the days of my life, to behold the beauty of the Lord. And to inquire in his temple.

For in the time of trouble he shall hide me in his pavilion: in the secret of his tabernacle shall he hide me; he shall set me upon a rock.

And now shall mine head be lifted above mine enemies round about me: therefore, will I offer in his tabernacle sacrifices of joy; I will sing, yea, I will sing praises unto the Lord.

Hear, O Lord, when I cry with my voice: have mercy also upon me and answer me.

When thou sad, seek ye my face; my heart said unto thee, thy face, Lord will I seek.

Hide not thy face far from me; put not thy servant away in anger: thou hast been my help; leave me not, neither forsake me, O God of my salvation.

When my mother and my father forsake me, then the Lord will take me up.

Teach me thy way, O Lord, and lead me in a plain path, because of my enemies.

Deliver me not over unto the will of my enemies: for false witnesses are revolted against me, and such as breath out cruelty.

I had fainted unless I had believed to see the goodness of the Lord in the land of the living.

WAIT ON THE LORD: BE OF GOOD COURAGE, AND HE SHALL STRENGTHEN THINE HEART: WAIT I SAY, ON THE LORD.

The song writer says how can he love me so, Lord I will never, never, know. To know God is to Love God for all his wonderful works and his great and mighty acts that he has performed in the earth. For the Lord is good to his people. You must allow yourself a chance to get to know who God really is, and what he can do. Many people do not allow themselves a chance to get to know who God really is. First thing most people do is set in judgement as to where there is no God, and if that is the case you have set yourself up for failure in the world already. Because his word has already told us that we cannot do nothing without God. And with that has been said where do you think you are going in life without God. Who do you think that you are going to accomplish things in life without God? Please give yourself that chance to get to know who God is before you make that reality call. I have been single for a long time without any man to help me in this life. If it had not been for God, I would not have known where I would be right to this day. Everything I got everything I own it was God that did it for me. I raised four adopted children on my own, because of God. Been in the Ministry for forty years, and traveled all over the country for forty years, it was not I it was God, that did it. I will not take the credit for something God did. I did not know a many of times which way to go, what do I do next, how do I get out of this situation and so forth, I want you to know that it was God. Many women in ministry have husbands that carried their load. Well, I want you to know that I am sixty-two years of age, and God has carried my load for me. I am an independent woman with the help and support of the Lord. For God has carried me for sixty-two years of my life. I never thought for the life of me I would be to be an adult and single for all these years and was able to do the things that I did for forty-three years. To know God is to love God. God is extra extraordinary to me. For I have found a friend in Jesus, in whom bear all my burdens, and my sins and griefs to bear, it is a privilege to carry everything to God in prayer. For God has been a lawyer for me in the court room, and he has been a shield and a buckler in the time of my distress. The song writer says I cannot give up know, I come to far from where I started from, but nobody told me that the road would be easy, I just cannot believe that he bought me this far, to leave me. God does not leave us, we leave him, because of our lack of faith and our clack of confidence in God. When you do not have the faith and the confidence to believe that he can carry you through anything and all things, you get up and walk away from God and go back to the world in which there is no help, especially in man. Things are not going to be easy all the time, you must prepare your heart to be able to endure your trials and tribulations. For we will have trouble in this life, but we must know that God is standing right by us to see us through. Sometimes in my life the battle got too strong for me to handle, I had to pull back and allow God to fight for me in that battle. I have come to a point in this life as to where God is concern, Lord, I will trust you. You have been too good to me to just get up and throw in the towel. Many times, I wanted to throw in the towel, but every time I started to throw in the towel God stepped right in and lifted me up.

PSALMS 29: 1-2 KJV

Give unto the Lord, O ye mighty, give unto the Lord glory and strength.

Give unto the Lord the glory due unto his name; worship the Lord in the beauty of Holiness.

I find that being in the ministry for forty years, and all the traveling that I have done and the things that I have seen, I can honestly say that there is a reality in serving a true and a living God. I have seen so many people out in the world that has been strung out on drugs and alcohol, and most of them do not have hope for today nor tomorrow. I find that the decisions that you make in your young days determine the outcome in your old age. Many have made the wrong decisions, and the outcome has been devastating. Some comes back and make a change, and some do not make it to be able to change their situation. This is the reason why I titled this book life on the streets without God and education. For there is a penalty that you must pay for not using common sense and exercising good judgement in your youth. Because God has told us to.

ECCLESIASTES 12:1-2 KJV

REMEMBER *now thy Creator in the days of thy youth, while the evil days come not, nor the years draw nigh, when thou shalt say, I have no pleasure in them.*

While the sun, nor the light, or the moon, or the stars, be not darkened, nor the clouds return after the rain:

You see by you serving God in your youth, it shall bring long life to you in the end. Do not wait to you get old and want to serve the Lord. Some do not make it to get old. And some in up in situations they can't not get out of. We as parents ought to take our children to church as children so that they can be taught of the Lore at an early age.

PSALMS 119:164-168

Seven times a day do I praise thee because of thy righteous judgement.

Great peace have they which love thy law: and nothing shall offend them.

Lord I have hoped for thy salvation and have done thy commandments.

My soul has kept thy testimonies; and I love them exceedingly.

I have kept thy precepts and thy testimonies: for all my ways are before thee.

For to know God is to love God. For he is great above all my expectations. I have tried God and I find that whenever I all on him he is always right there for me. Without God In my life, I would not have made it this far. For I have come this far by faith, leaning, and standing on the word of God. I have experience so much jealous and hatred among people because of my faith in him. I had to come into the knowledge as to where it was not me, they were hating it was the spirit of God that was dwelling down on the inside. But what they did not know that in order to be like me you have to give up the things that I had to give up. And not many people are willing to give up the wrong things in life for the right things in life. It takes a lifelong of sacrifices to become like Jesus. And it is not an easy task to do. Because you cannot do things like the people that is in the world. Because I gave up everything in the natural rim, to gain the things in the spiritual rim. Therefore, when we walk in the spirit, we will not be able to fulfill the lust of the flesh. And the people that are not saved, do not understand the life you surrendered. I surrendered my life on my own, no one put a gun to my head and make me get saved for forty-three years. I surrendered me on my own free will. And that goes for everyone else God do not force us to serve him, he gives us a choice, and it is up to us to choose what choice we are going to make. He gave the children of Israel a choice, and the gentiles. If you choose God, you choose long life and prosperity, and all the other good things that come with in serving a true and a living god.

I am experiencing good help know that I am sixty-two years of age. I am still able to do the things that I did in my teenage days. I jog, exercise for hours, and I still do not get tired. That is the price you pay for being obedient, and the price you pay for serving a true and a living God. Having God in your life helps you to overcome the bad things and habit that is poisoning this present world. The drugs and the alcohol, cigarettes, having sex out of wedlock, having all these children, and no father to take care of the. These are the things that God hates. And many people have chose to walk in these things instead of serving God. For there is a reality in serving a true and a living God. For to know God is to love God. Jesus said if you love me, you will keep my commandments.

And they thirsted not when he led them through the dessert: he caused the waters to flow out of the rock for them: he clave the rock also, and the waters gushed out.

There is no peace, saith the Lord, unto the wicked.

PSALMS 1:1-6

Blessed is the man that walked not in the counsel of the ungodly, nor stands in the way of sinners, nor sits in the seat of the scornful.

ISAIAH 48:21-22

But his delight is in the law of the Lord; and in his law doth he meditates day and night.

And he shall be like a tree planted by the rivers of water, that bringeth forth his fruit in his season; his leaf also shall not wither; and whatever he doth shall prosper.

The ungodly is not so: but are like the chaff which the wind drives away.

Therefore, the ungodly shall not stand in the judgement, nor sinners in the congregation of the righteous.

For the Lord, the way of the righteous: but the way of the ungodly shall perish.

PROVERBS 20:27-30.

The spirit of a man is the candle of the Lord, searching all the inward parts of the belly.

Mercy and truth preserve the king: and his throne is up holden by mercy.

The glory of young men is their strength: and the beauty of old men is the grey head.

God sent his son into the world not to condemn the world but that the world might be saved through his son.

For his son gave his life to as many as would believe on him, and that they should not perish but have everlasting life. Jesus said let whosoever will let him come and eat of the tree of life freely, and drink from the fountain of life. We have choices, and choices have consequences.

You can choose God and live, or you can choose the world and die. Your chose.

ECCLESIASTES 9:1-2

For all this I considered in my heart even to declare all this, that the righteous, and the wise, and their works, are in the hand of God: no man knows either love or hatred by all that is before them.

All things come alike to all: there is one event to the righteous, and to the wicked; to the good and to the clean, and to the unclean; to him that sacrifices, and to him that sacrificed not: as is the good, so is the sinner; and he that swears, as he that fears an oath.

PSALMS 121: 1-

I will lift mine eyes unto the hills, from whence comes my help.

My help comes from the Lord, which made heaven and earth.

He will not suffer thy foot to be moved: he that keeps thee will not slumber.

Behold he that keeps Israel shall neither slumber nor sleep.

The Lord is thy keeper: The Lord is thy shade upon thy right hand.

The sun shall not smite thee by day, nor the moon by night.

The Lord shall preserve the from all evil: he shall preserve thy soul.

The Lord shall preserve thy going out and thy coming in from this time forth, and even for ever-more.

FOR TO KNOW GOD IS TO LOVE GOD

CHAPTER-ELEVEN

EVERYTHING AROUND YOU FAIL WHERE DO YOU GO AND TO WHOM DO YOU TURN TO

Many are the afflictions of the righteous; but the Lord delivereth him out of them all.

PSALMS 34:19KJV

When Everything Around You Fail Where do you go And to whom do you turn to

Sometimes in this life, we are going to have trials and tribulations and trouble on every side. But the Lord Jesus lets us know that we don't have to be afraid, just as he came down and overcame the world, we can overcome too. The word of the Lord tells us, that when we have done all, we can do to stand; stand therefore anyhow. Many of the afflictions of the righteous; but the Lord will deliver us out of them all. I have been through trial after trial, and there seems to be no relief in sight, but one thing I had to constantly do is to continue to pray. Because without that prayer in my life, I wouldn't have made it this far. For that, we do know that the prayers of a righteous man availed much. God hears the cry of the righteous. I remember a dream I had back in 2002, and it was concerning when a tornado came through my house and tore it down. The dream disturbed me because deep down in my spirit I knew trouble was coming, but I didn't think that it would have been as bad as it was. After the dream, the enemy came in like a flood and tore my entire household into turmoil. All the children walked out of the house and put themselves into the system. I am reminded that the devil can't do anything to you and your family unless he gets permission from God. Just like Job, the devil had to get permission from God to put his hands against Jo and his family, and all his substances. So, I was aware that God had given the devil permission to come in and tear everything up. So, after everybody left, I gave everybody's belongings to other children in the community, I packed my belongings and my mother's belongings and put them in storage in Indianapolis Indiana, and my mother and I headed back to St. Louis. From that point, I didn't realize how tired and stressed out I was. So, I stayed there for a few months sleeping, because I was so tired, after being in the Ministry at an early age, the many trials had taken a toll on me. And I just needed to rest a while. I rested and I headed down the road to Tampa Bay, Florida. I got a driving job driving charter buses. I was there for about one year. I got a chance to go to Disney World every week free of charge, because I held a CDL license, and the groups we took down there took care of us very well. And the days I didn't work I hung out on the beach with my ramp floating. While I was there in St. Petersburg Florida, there were four hurricanes, one after the other, then I heard the voice of the Lord saying pack up and go home. Which was back in East St. Louis Illinois. I didn't want to leave but I had to. On one of my trips driving to Disney World, we in in a convoy, and the head of the group was a seventy-five-year-old male. When we get to Disney and discharge all the passengers off the bus, we all get on the elderly gentleman's bus and go for breakfast. So, the guy started cursing at me talking crazy with racial comments, so I asked what was wrong with you. So, I wouldn't talk to him anymore. So, we arrived at the restaurant, we went inside, and he started cursing at one of the waiters, so I asked the other young lady that was with me what was wrong with the dude, and she replied he was a racist. So, I told him not to say anything else to me because once I get back to the office, I will be reporting him for his racist remarks and sexual harassment comments. I became so stressed out on that trip that I just couldn't wait until I got back to St. Petersburg Florida. When I got back and parked my bus, I went inside and made a report on him for his behavior, they called him into the office reprimanded him, and told him he better not ever go near me again. So, he got angry and told the other drivers about what I had reported, so they all started treating me crazy. So, the following week, I got sick and didn't show up for work, so I called in and told them I was sick, and I was unable to drive. The next day, late in the evening I went to the job to drop off my money bag, and the office and the parking lot were full of people. I was a little scared to go in, so I said let me go in anyway. Once I got In, the manager called me into the office and said you know we have had a death in the company, I replied no I didn't know, who is it I replied he said Jim, I asked if it was Jim that had been cursing at me down in Disney World, he replied yes, he is the one. My heart almost jumped out of my chest. So, I asked him how he died. He replied that the driver was coming back from AM Track in Fort Lauderdale and fell dead while he was behind the wheel of a commercial bus. After his head hit the steering wheel, a passenger ran up and jumped in the seat because the driver had fallen into the stairwell of the front door. This bus was carrying twenty-seven elderly people who had just returned from a cruise and were on their way back home to Tampa Bay Florida. One of the passengers was a retired nurse and the passenger that got behind the wheel to steer the bus was her husband. Another passenger calls AM Track to get information on how to stop that bus. The bus was going up on the St Petersburg bridge, and after you get to the top the bridge drops and starts a down drop. After the driver fall dead, the bus hits the bridge about three times, am track gave the information to one of the passengers to pull the yellow knob down on the left side of their left leg, and that will put the brakes on. Thank God everyone was saved. But do you see your enemy will be God's enemy?

God will protect his people at all costs. No weapon is formed against us that will prosper. And every tongue that rises against us in judgment shall be condemned. From 2002 until 2014, I was in a battle that long, I didn't know if I was going to make it out with my sanity. Then I left Florida and had to go home. The Lord said that he needed me to go home because he was getting ready to take my mother. So, I went home and stayed with her, I was so stressed out because I had not been home since I left East St. Louis at the age of nineteen. And I already knew that my trials were going to get harder being there, because of the jealousy and the animosity that the family feels against. So, I'm back at home, and the drama starts, and it was bad, very bad, I have brothers that like to fight with me and the other brothers. The devil will do all he can to turn you away from following God. The devil is so cruel that he will have you thinking that God is allowing all this trouble to come upon you, and he is nowhere to be found. But through all my trials and tribulations, and when everything around me fails, and it looks like there is no hope, I can truly say you must keep your hands in God's hand. When you feel like giving up, just remember this one thing the darkest hour is just before dawn. When everything around you fail, family and friends turn their back on you, no other help I know but to call upon the name of the Lord. And it appears to be no ending in sight, when everything around me has failed, and my world has been turned upside down. Then I had to remember what David said, for I will lift my eyes, unto the hills from whence cometh my help, all my help comes from the Lord, the maker of heaven and earth. I lost my job, I lost my home, and cars, and family and friends turned against me, and church folk turned against me and lied to me. In Jul 2005 my mother passed away, I was more confused and lost than ever before because me and my mother traveled together for over twenty years. She was my babysitter. I had become deeper into depression than ever before, I slept woke up, go back to sleep. I woke up sad, I went to sleep sad, I walked around all day sad. Wondering when will my help arrive. Lord where are you, I need help, so I sat there in that frame of mind until deliverance came. I got up one day to go out to my car, and I was standing under a tree, and a white feather fell on the top of my head. That was a sign that help was on its way. I went back in the house got on the couch and fell asleep and I saw the Lord, he picked me up and he began to hold me in his arms, then he started rocking me. The peace of God came over me until I just fell asleep in the arms of the Lord. I heard him speak and said your time is not up, I need you to go back and complete your mission. So, I said OK Lord. Then I awakened and I could still feel the peace of God. I got back up and started pressing on a little bit further. I am reminded of when John the Baptist baptized Jesus when the spirit of the Lord ascended upon him like a dove. And then God spoke and told them that this is my beloved son, whom I am well pleased with, hear ye him. My strength had been renewed, my joy had been restored when I went to church, I couldn't stop shouting, because I knew that the joy of the Lord was my strength. I was In St. Louis Mo. At that time, I knew I had a little time left before I retired, so I wanted to retire on the outskirts of Chicago, or the state line of Indiana. I waited patiently for the Lord, and he heard my cry. In June of 2014, I made my move to Indiana and got a job as a Mega Bus driver located in Chicago, Illinois. I waited for ten years before God gave me the ok to make the move. It appeared to look like everything I tried to do failed. When you are a born-again Christian, the devil will fight you tooth and nail, he will intervene in everything you try to do that is good. That's the devil's job to stop you from prospering and to hinder you on the assignment God has assigned to you. Just as Jesus overcame, we can overcome also. The devil stays on his job twenty-four-seven, and we need to be consistent in praying twenty-four-seven so that the old devil will not get an advantage over us. No matter how hard the task gets, Jesus told the disciples that I must work the work of him that sent me, while its day, the night cometh when no man can work. John 9:4.

While we are healthy, enclose within our right mind, got our health and strength, we need to do what we can for the Lord, while it is day, because when night time comes you cannot work. Don't wait until you get down on your sick bed of affliction, when some type of sickness or illness has taken hold, then you are wishing you had a worked for the Lord before you got down and out. You must work while its day, because when you think about it in the natural, at dark you can't see nothing, you need a flashlight to see where you are going. Because while you are walking in the dark you are most likely to stumble and fall. You won't be able to work when you have fallen ill are some type of sickness takes over your body. There is an old saying that he may not come when you want him, but he is always on time. For the Lord Jesus has promised us that he will never leave us or forsake us. If darkness never comes into our lives, how do we know that Jesus can deliver up like he promised. How do we know that Jesus is a healer if we have never been sick, if we never had a need how do we know that he will meet every need? Just as Jesus came in and paid that price, hung, bleed suffer, beaten, spit on, lied on strips across his back, and yet he opened not his mouth, and said not a mumbling word. To live Godly in the Lord we must arm our self to suffer like wise. The Lord has told us in his Holy word, that when we go through the fire we will not be burned, when the waters over shadow us we will not drown. Our fallers and our trials are for our own learning, and a testimony for others who you are going to meet that might be going through the same thing that God bought you out of. When everything around you fail, we can look to the hills from whence comes our help, knowing that our help, knowing that our help comes from the Lord the maker of heaven and earth.

From 2004 until 2014 the devil tried his best to take my mind, not only my mind he has tried to kill me from the age of 16 up until now. And I can truly say that it was nobody but God that withstood the hand of the enemy, and made him get back, and leave me alone and stopped him from taking me out. In my walk with God, I had to know him for myself. Ten years is a long time to go through a storm, and early one morning I was in a dream, and I saw the Lord standing between heaven and the earth, I was so sad because the battle was too strong for me, I thought that I have fought my best, and I didn't feel like fighting anymore. And when I saw Jesus, he looked down at me smiling, his hand was folded in the front of him, and his wings came out into the front of him, and I spoke to him and I said Jesus that you and I were smiling, I looked around and all my enemies were in behind me, and I heard the voice of the Lord say Grab hold. The people that were behind me to do me harm were people that I knew. The Lord's wigs came from in the back of him, into a praying hands position, then he spoke and said My Friend grab hold, I went to grab hold of his wing in a praying hands position, and before I could touch his wing, his power picked me up, out of the midst of my enemies and sat me down to a safe location, away from my enemies. He appeared to me three times and took me out of the midst of my enemies, and he left and went back and sat on the throne. I looked around again and here my enemies started chasing me again, I looked for Jesus for the fourth time, and he put an unusual gun in my hands, and I heard his voice again, he said I came down three times to deliver you, I want you to use what I have put in your hands, and he replied I'm not coming down no more. I looked at the gun he had put in my hand, and the barrel of the gun was as big as my hand. My enemies were approaching me fast, I walked up to the first one and I told him to open your mouth, he opened his mouth, I stuck the barrel of the gun in his mouth and I fired it. It was not bullets that came from that gun, it was white smoke, and after I fired it that person disappeared, and vanished into thin air. And I shot about five more people with that gun, they all vanished into thin air. I knew who the people were that was in that vision. Therefore, we shouldn't put our hands and mouth against people, especially when we don't know who they are. When God knew that I had been battled by the storms of life, it took me down, but it didn't take me out. God's power is so great I didn't even have to touch his wings, before I could touch his wing his power had already picked me up and sat me down in a safe place away from my enemies. In real life I see my enemies disappearing one by one and name by name. If I had never gone through the storm, how would I know that God is a deliverer? When everything around you fail, that's when God steps in, when you have done all, you can do then the Lord God Almighty steps in and lets us know we can't do nothing, but it is he that grants us grace and mercy, and it is him that keeps his arm of protection around us to stop the enemy from destroying us before our time. God wants us to learn how to trust in him, and no one else, in good times and in the bad times. When we try to do things on our own, he allows things to fail, because we need to learn how to put our trust completely in him and not in man. And I find out that when everything around you have failed, he steps in a day and corrects everything you have been going through for years. That's why we as a people of God must learn how to lean on and depend upon God. God is omnipotent, there are many Gods, but there is only one true and living God. God wants the glory for everything he does for us in our lives. That's why he allows everything around us to fail because he does not want us to get the glory, the glory does not belong to us, it belongs to God. We should not be praising ourselves; all glory and honor is due unto the Lord. God has spoken in his word; My glory will I not give to another; nor will I give praises to graven images. There are many Gods, but there is only one true and living God. If we can just only try to hold on and keep the faith, I heard the words of the Lord saying stand still and see the salvation of the Lord. We must endure for a season, and when that season is up, it's time to get built back up because down the road trouble is coming again. So, we need to be built back up in prayer, fasting, and consecration. And most of the time when you start going through the storm again, it usually doesn't be the same trial and tribulation that you came out of. And most trials don't last the same, some short some long, and when I mean long it can last for years. One thing that I found out is that tribulation comes for a reason, I can use myself for instance, I was in very dire need of patience, and I went through a trial for ten years, patience began to manifest itself throughout my life after I came out of that storm. But I'm still in need of some more. I just came out of another trial from 2017 to 2020, November fifteen the storm in my life became calm again. This time patience is having her perfect work in me. We must look unto the Lord when everything around us has failed, there is no other help I know. I have been saved for forty-three years and darkness has come into my life many times. And sometimes I was in a position where I couldn't pray because I was so overstricken with grief. The only thing I could do was to go and lay before the Lord until help came. Some of the trials and tribulations have been so devastating that there was nothing for me to do but lay before God and wait for deliverance to take place. I have truly experienced the hand of God and God's power of deliverance, even when I had lost hope in some very tough situations. He showed up and then he showed out. Strong and mighty did he show up, and then he spoke to me and said trust me didn't not I tell you that I will be with you, in the fire, and in the flood, down in the valley, and upon the mountain top. God has truly shown me the greatness of his power. I experience him bringing me out with a mighty strong hand. If God be for you, who can be against you? And if God be for you that's more than the whole world against you.

When I first got saved no one told me that the road would be easy, and neither did tell me that I was going to hit many rough spots on the journey. When I first got saved, I remember every time I went through something I complained to God, asking him why I had to go through this. I thought everything would be easier than being out in the world. I was complaining because I did not understand what was happening to me. So, I started doing a lot of fasting and praying, and I didn't know why. I would go down to the Church and lock myself in from Friday to Sunday with no food or water, and I didn't understand why, but down the road, my heart began to understand. On my journey, I married an unsaved man who put me through hell. I didn't know that he had gotten mixed up with those drug dealers. He started stealing, running off with them people drugs, he almost got me killed in my own house, stealing people drugs, thinking he slick. I preached to the drug man who was trying to take over my house, and I told him to get out and take him with me, and I don't ever want to see you back in my house again. I told him that whatever you must do to get your money back take it out on his hide outside, and not in here. I told him I was in the ministry and I never had a problem with the dope man again. It's been forty-three years now and Satan has not defeated me yet. There is no defeat in God. If you get defeated in God that's because you were not trying, and you just wanted to give up and go back out into a world of sin. Through all the fasting and praying my anointing became greater, my discernment became more clearer, I could see people for just what they were. I was able to recognize that the devil was trying to kill me and get me on drugs and alcohol. But God that had me doing all that fasting and praying withstood me. And he kept me until I was able to get up and walk on my own.

Oh, but God withstood him and he didn't leave me in the hands of the enemy. For he bought me, and he taught me, and he fought for me when I couldn't fight for myself being a newborn babe in the Ministry. When you find yourself in a position where you can't pray, trials and tribulations have become overwhelming we must learn how to stand still and see the salvation of the Lord. I had to come into the knowledge of the devil, and that his motive is to turn us around, and to stop us from following God. The devil lost his reward when he got kicked out of heaven. God has already spoken and said my Glory will I not give unto another, neither will I give praises to graven images. So, when he was in heaven, the director of the choir he lusted after the Glory that God had. He lost out, and the bible states that when God kicked him out of heaven, he convinced a third of the angels to follow him in coming against the highest. The Bible tells us when God kicked him out, he beheld satin as lightning falling.

Satan lost out and he wants you to lose out as well. The devil is an accuser of the brethren, he goes before God Day and night accusing you before our God. That's why when trouble comes stand your ground, wait on God, and see the salvation of the Lord. For the Lord will make the devil behave himself, for God has given us the power to rebuke him in the name of Jesus. We must realize that even the devil and his angels fear and tremble at the name of Jesus. So, if the devil and his fallen angels tremble and fear in the name of Jesus, what about man? You find people walking around this earth with no fear of nothing and nobody. We must have some type of fear in this world because if we don't, we will do just about anything, that's not about Holiness. The only thing the devil has is a big bark, but he has no teeth to bite. Before Jesus went to the cross, he told the disciples that he was going away, and he replied except that seed be put in the ground and die, there will be no redemption for sin. For he must go away; and come back again, for Jesus died and for three days Jesus was in the heart of the earth. He gave those who had already died a chance to have eternal life. For three days he whooped the devil, and on that third day, he rose just like he said he would. Then when he rose, he let us know I have the key now to eternal life, then he replied all power has been given unto me over heaven and earth. For what the prophets could not accomplish, because no man was worthy, the flesh could not complete this task. It took God creating himself a son to come down to redeem us from the power of death, in which Adam and Eve sinned and caused death for everybody.

For what the father sent him to do he completed the mission. Mary Magdalene was the first person he had appeared to. And then he told her to go tell my brethren.

That I have ascended unto my Father and your Father, and to my God and your God.

Then he replied that all power has been given unto me. But because he lives, we can face tomorrow, and because he got up from the grave, with all power we can make it to the end as well. When he died, he imparted that same power into our mortal bodies, because he knew that we were going to need that same power to be able to live on this earth and perform the work God has ordained us to do, we can't do the work without the power, it would be on non-effect. We have no excuse now not to live for God and hold on to our prayers and our faith in God. Because faith in God knows no defeat. For he has given us the power to overcome every obstacle that gets in our way. For every complaint, and excuse has been taken to the cross. The enemy comes to shake your faith, he huffs and puffs to make us scared of him. But the power of the Holy Ghost, along with intercessory prayer, fasting, and consecration, is the only thing that keeps us holding on to God's unchanging hands.

When it looks like everything around you have failed, and it seems like you want to give up and throw in the towel, look up knowing that your redemption draws nigh.

Keep in mind that the trying of your faith worketh patience; So, let patience have her perfect work.

When Life troubles seems to get you down
Just call on Jesus he is always around
When you can't seem to find you way
Go into your secret closet and pray
God will answer you on today
And let you know that help is on its way.

CHAPTER-TWELVE

WHERE THERE IS NO LOVE THERE IS NO RESPECT

Be not deceived for God is not marked, for whatsoever that a man soweth, that shall he also reap:

Galatians 6:7 KJV

For he that soweth to his flesh, shall of the flesh reap corruption; for he that soweth to the Spirit, shall of the spirit reap life everlasting.

In addition, let us not be weary in well doing: for in due season we shall reap, if we faint not.

As we have therefore opportunity, let us do well unto all men, especially unto them who are of the household of faith.

Galatians 6: 8-10

We are living in a day and time where the word of the Lord teaches us that in the last days, man shall be lovers of themselves, rather than lovers of God. In addition, because iniquity has abounded, the love of many has waxed cold. We are living in a day and age where there is no love anywhere. Man speaks that he loves you from his mouth, but his heart is far from it. Anybody can say that, they love you but turn around the next second and talk about you as if you were nothing. They will gossip and lie to you and turn right back around and tell you that they love you. For you to walk around with a double tongue and a forward mouth, you have no love neither do you have any respect. Where there is no love, there is no respect. Because love will not allow you to lie to your brother or sister. Neither will it allow you to harm a person you are supposed to have love and respect for. Even in our own families, there is no love nor is there any respect. In addition, these things ought not to be said by the Lord. Then I also had to deal with the disrespect of the church, and this ought not to be. If you are to represent The Love of God, you must show it every day of your life, not only on Sundays but every day of the week. Not only to the household of faith but also to your blood family. You do not go around in the world and treat strangers better than you treat your own family; this should not be. We have the word of God mixed up. How can we profess that we love God and hate our sister and brother, the word of God says we are a liar, and the truth is not in us. Your works speak for you, so therefore do not allow your mouth to say one thing, and your actions are doing something very different. You must allow your thoughts and your actions to work together. So, that you will not be held in contempt when the Lord Jesus shall appear, and we must stand before the Great White Throne to give an account of every deed that was done in this body. Learn how to be righteous in everything that you do. Jesus had given the disciples a command: And that commandment was for them to love ye one another, as I have loved you. When you possess the Love of God, you will not intentionally hurt people because of your Ill intentions, and the jealousy that rules you from the inside. Jealousy, hatred, envy, and strife cause you to harm people for no good reason. We find many family members fighting all the time, maybe one has a little bit more than the other, and if that's the case why not try to help the one that doesn't have it don't have to be money at all the time, maybe they need personal things now and then. In addition, most of the time they do not know what they are fighting about. In addition, the disrespect goes on for years. We must remember that when things like that take place in a family, that is a generational curse. In addition, somebody must be strong enough and have enough Love for God in them to stand against, the wicked devices of the devil. Jealousy, hatred envy, and strife, talking against your sister and your brother for no good reason is of the devil. We did not hear about Jesus talking against the disciples one to another. So why are we going around spreading people's business across the country, most of the time it's just gossip and lies, because where there is no love there is no respect. Love and respect will cause you to do the right thing by all men because Love and respect are of God. After family members have been disrespectful to one another for years and years, then when one has passed away, and you did not make amends with them, then it is on your conscious for the rest of your life. This is why you have to treat everybody with Love and respect, so that when something does happen you can say they you have done your best, and you don't have to worry about not being able to sleep at night because of the disrespect that you have shown them down through the years. Where there is no Love there is no respect, how can you have Love for someone and do not have respect for him or her? How can you say that you love God and hate your sister and your brother, for you are a liar, and the truth is not in you, because you see them every day, and you do not have any love for them nor do you have any respect for them? However, God is a Spirit, we pray to someone that we do not see, but we say that we Love God, and people the things ought not to be. Love ye one another as Christ has loved us. For we know that we are in the last days, and because we are in the last days, the love of many has waxed cold. More and more each day, we see mother against daughter, daughter against mother, father against son, son against father, sister against sister, brother against brother. Where there is no love there is no respect.

I raised four adopted children from small children, and as they started growing into adolescence, their attitude and their personality started coming out, we must realize that what is on the inside of you is going to start to show on the outside of you. The disrespect started coming out, so therefore by you showing me how disrespectful you are, I knew then that they did not have any love for me. Because if they did, Love does not have you being disrespectful to the person who has adopted you and caring for you, where there is no love there is no respect. They started openly rebellion and dared me to say anything to them. Well, I am the type of person I am not going to allow you to run over me in my house. They started doing things to deliberately aggravate me, they knew the things that would make me mad. Just like my oldest nephew, every time I leave home, I would give them chores to do, after I'm gone, he tells them that they don't have to do anything I said because I was nobody's mother, where there is no love, there is no respect. I took those children to church every Sunday, and I cannot understand for the life of me how they turned out the way that they did. I was sad for many days, about their life. However, there was nothing that I could do or say to make them believe will get better. I heard the voice of the Lord say that all the children were leaving. And he told me that they were going to be scattered all over the country, and he said when he got done punishing them for their behavior, and for the disrespect that they had committed against me in my own home, they would be back to ask for forgiveness. I put the oldest nephew out for staying out in the streets all night long thinking that he could walk in my house anytime he wanted to and started drinking and using drugs. I was not getting ready to tolerate that out of nobody's children, so I showed him the door, I sent him to East St. Louis, Illinois to my mother's house, and from there he went to the military, and got beat up, and kicked out because of no respect for his Superior Officers. Where there is no love there is no respect. His life started going downhill from there. After taking them to church every Sunday people would give me high praises on how well-mannered these children were, but they did not know the hidden secret about them outside of church, and inside of my home. However, God knew and he was not going to allow me to be deceived in my own home. They would get up to testify, and thank the Lord for giving them a family that cared about them and loved them, that was all a lie, where there is no love there is no respect. It wounded me so badly to take someone else's child in my house, and because of one bad apple that was in the basket, it caused the whole basket of apples to get rotten. My God help us today, to walk circumspectly, not as fools, but as wise. For we will in this life reap everything we have sown, whether it has been good, or whether it has been evil. So, the Lord put an end to it all they all walked out and left, my thought was if you can do a better job for yourself at the age of thirteen and fifteen, I recommend that you keep moving and try to do the best you can for yourself. I was only trying to teach them how to survive. Anytime your biological parents allow you to go to foster care and do not even try to come back and get you, nor even try to contact you. Why would you want to be adopted? In addition, you have shown nothing but disrespect in the adopted mother's home. When your biological parents gave you up and walked away. Where there is no love there is no respect, you must learn to have respect for the one that is taking care of you, because the one that is taking care of have to have some type of love for you for them to adopt you and allow you to live in their home until you were grown. Clothes, shoes, food, and raiment were provided for you, and when you look back there was nothing that you needed, everything was provided for you including a nice clean home where there was not much for you to do except to keep your living quarters clean, and you didn't even want to do that. School fees were paid every semester, new uniforms were bought every school year, lunches were provided, and you got an allowance, I allowed you to earn extra money, what more could I have done, I was not appreciated for all that I did for everybody, because where there is no love there is no respect. I am sorry you walked out and had to go through what you are going through, but I could not allow you to run over me in my house. We all make mistakes, but after we realize that we have made a huge mistake, we need to learn how to ask God to forgive us and ask that person we have so wronged for forgiveness so that we can have a piece of mind behind the behavior you exercised. Sometimes when we are young the devil makes us think that the grass is greener on the other side of the fence, when you cross over that fence and get to the other side, you find that the grass has not been watered, and the temperature of the sun has scorched the grass until it has died. In addition, know the guilt sets in, you see that the grass is not so green on the other side of the fence. However, you still do not dare to humble yourself and ask for forgiveness. Where there is no love, there is no respect. I was even threatened by one of them with the cops, so I had to paddle her for her behavior, I was only trying to bring her up in a way, so she could be wise and not let men trick her, and get all those kids, and end up taking care of them on her own. Therefore, they thought my teaching was wrong I had to allow them to go where they were going and do a better job for themselves than I was doing. What do you know at the age of thirteen, nothing, where there is no love there is no respect? So, after I had been threatened by the police, I told her she had one more time to open her mouth to me in my home, she waited for about three months, and she did it again, I patted her again, and then she had the nerve to talk crazy to me in front of company. I patted her right in front of the company, and I told her if the company did not like it, they could get some too. After the company left, I went upstairs and dealt with her again, because I saw that she had gotten out of hand, so I told them to get their clothes ready for tomorrow, and on Monday, I called children's services. I had warned her that when she came home on Monday children's services were going to be waiting on her. Well, someone set the clock early that morning, so I got up and went downstairs on the couch, and waited for them to get dressed and have their breakfast; I wanted to make sure she did not sneak any clothes out of the house. My motto was you came with nothing and you will leave with nothing period. Therefore, after they left for school, I called children's services to report her behavior and to let them know that she could not continually live in my house talking to me crazy, like she was the momma and I was her child that will never happen in my world. So, when I called them, they told me Ms. Scruggs if she doesn't show back up at home, this is what I want you to do, call the police and put a warrant on her, then take her down to the courthouse before the judge, then I replied ok I surely would. I decided not to go to school, that particular day, and I lay waiting on the coach, about three-fifteen of the other two kids came home, but she did not.

Therefore, I called the police to come to the house, and I made a runaway report on her. In addition, later that night she still did not show up. I felt her presence around the apartment complex, and then I knew that she was in the area. Therefore, the next day I asked the other two kids to go to the office and call me if she shows back up at school. Therefore, I was lying across my bed and I was in a deep dream, and she was in the dream, and I saw her standing, and she had on her faded jeans, white T-shirt, and white sneakers. So, the phone rang and it was her sister, so all three of the children were in the same grade, and they had a class together, so she called me to let me know that Jasmine showed up at school. I told her thanks for calling I was on my way. I got dressed and called the police on my way out the door. So, Huber Heights police met me at the school, and they went into her classroom and escorted her out, I asked them If they could escort her down there because if she opened her mouth to me again while she was in my car, I'm going to pull the car over and get her again. Therefore, they explained to me that they were not allowed to transfer children down to the courthouse anymore. I asked the officer if he could talk to her about not opening her mouth, so the officer took her to the back room and told her something, but I did not hear what the officer had told her, because when she came out of the room she was screaming and crying. Where there is no love, there is no respect, when someone opens their mouth up to you and speaks whatever comes to their mind, and doesn't care how they say it, a child is supposed to be taught, and no child is supposed to be teaching the parents. I headed down to the courthouse took her in and registered her, we then had to go into the intake room to give our statement. After giving our statement, they called in Children Services to come, and then Children Services called up an emergency foster parent. The foster parent arrives and she falls out in the middle of the floor and begins screaming, I told her that you should have thought about that before you started opening your mouth to me, and you thought that you were going to get away with it. I warned them so many times that this was going to happen if they tried running over me in my house. I walked out of the courthouse and left her right there. Unit three days later, we had to go before the Judge. I showed up at court three days later she was there with her new foster parent, and children services. We were asked to go into the courtroom, and her attorney was present because the judge told Children Services to get her a lawyer. Therefore, we went back to court, and Children Services tried to get the judge to release the case. From his courtroom and send it over to the guardianship court. In addition, the Judge asked me, if I wanted to send the case to the other court or try the case in his courtroom. I replied, judge due to all respect, I would like to keep the case here in your court. Therefore, he found her to be unruly and ungovernable. He put her on probation until she was eighteen. In addition, told her that he did not want to see her again in his courtroom. He told her how he was in his chambers watching her disrespect me in the courthouse and how she should have been thankful that somebody of my character had adopted her and her brother together. The judge told her that it is so many children that would love to have a mother like Ms. Scruggs. So many children out there who would never have a chance to be adopted, and you got an adoption placement and did not appreciate it. Therefore, the Judge asked Children Services what they were all going to do with her, and they replied that they were going to do an investigation on Ms. Scruggs and send her back. Where there is no love there is no respect. Because love does not have you disrespecting your elders. The Judge told the Children's services, no you are not going to put her back in Ms. Scruggs's home because Ms. Scruggs said that she could not come back to her home. He asked Children Services where she came from, they replied Hamilton County, I replied no she did not she came from Columbus, Ohio. The judge told them to go back and pull her file, find a long-lost uncle, and send her back to them. In addition, the judge said maybe down the road Ms. Scruggs can forgive her and they can make amends and get back together. I decided to move out of Dayton, Ohio, and move to Indianapolis. After I got into Indianapolis the brother and my niece decided to do the same thing that their sister did. I came home from work early one night and found my niece and her brother in my bedroom watching pornography on my computer. Therefore, I had to whip their butts. In addition, they had allowed all the children into my apartment, to eat up all the snacks and soda pops, and then trashed the house. Therefore, I made them clean it up, and the next night I came home early the next day, because I had gotten into an argument with someone on the job, and then walked out and quit. I came home again, and as I was driving up the street, I saw a light on the building across from my building. I looked up at my bedroom window, and the light was coming from my bedroom. As I parked the car, I was on the phone talking to my mother. In addition, I told her that they were in my bedroom again, and she said that I was lying, I told her to stay on the phone I was going to sneak up there and catch her again in my bedroom. I sneaked upstairs and walked into my bedroom, the boy was sitting in my computer chair, on my computer watching pornography. I stood in the back of him for a good minute, and he finally looked around, saw that it was me, humped up, and started screaming. I grabbed him and whipped his but, but the girl had been watching out for me she had already seen me out there and didn't warn him, she allowed him to take the wrap by himself. So, when I went to go to her room, she already had the door locked, with a chair behind it, I didn't even ask her to open the door, I proceeded and kicked it in and I prattled her about along with him. Therefore, I drove to St. Louis to pick up my mother to come back and watch the house. When my mother and I returned from St. Louis, she made the kids clean the house back up and made them eat peanut butter and jelly sandwiches. Where there is no love, there is no respect. So, on Monday morning both of the children went to school and one came home and the other did not get off the bus. He had ditched school and started running around with all those bad kids, setting around the apartment complex and setting off fire alarms in all the buildings. The sheriff kicked him up during the course of the night, and they came to my door with him in the back of the squad car and gave me a number to call and told me where he was taking him, and for me to call that number the next day. Therefore, the next day, I waited outside in the car. However, my mother and I when my niece came in from school, I told her to give me my keys and get into the van, then we went to the place where Roy was and I gave my statement, colleen went into a room and I never saw neither one of them again. Colleen and Roy said that they did not want to go back and live with that woman. Where there is no love, there is no respect, because respect will not allow you to have sex in your mother's bed. And love will not have you been evil towards someone who took time out of their busy schedule to adopt you and give you a permanent place to live, and that is the gratitude that you have toward them calling them in the courtroom that woman. Where there is no love there is no respect. So, both of them were placed into a residential center for three months, then we went to court, and they told so many lies against me until I did not have the strength nor the energy left to keep fighting against the evil that was present in my home. When Roy got on the stand, he addressed me as that woman, I looked at him and the Judge stepped in and said you listen up young man, don't you ever come into my courtroom and address someone as being that woman, he said if you don't want to call her your mother to address her as Ms. Scruggs. Therefore, after the trial, the judge ordered Children Services to find a foster home to put them in. Then the Judge asked me if I wanted visitations, I said no, because I did not put them there. Therefore, Colleen said that she did not want to go with Grandma. I told my mother to come on I left the courtroom, and I told my mother to take your time and walk, so, I ran out of the court house went and got my car, drove up to the door, and picked up my mother, and we left. I spent over twenty years raising adopted children which was so ungrateful and disrespectful. I find so many people in life that have gotten caught up in the system and people just had to let them go, because when you get to a point in life where nobody can tell you anything, then you are going to have to learn the hard way. That means everything you do is going to be complicated for you because you have refused to receive instructions. I did not get this far in life not accepting instructions. So, I have not seen them since, until this day. I had given up my dreams so that they may have a chance for education. I found out one thing in life you could not make a person take or accept the things that you want for them. I provided everything for them and it still was not enough for them. They walked away and in other words, they were telling me to kiss their butt, and that they did not need me, so, sad I was so hurt it took me a long time to get over that, and I am still not quiet over the matter yet. For where there is no love there is no respect. I did love the children. Nevertheless, I couldn't understand what I had done wrong to them, for me to allow them to live in my home. In addition, turn around and disrespect me the way that they did. Going through the storm it made me stronger. It also opened up my eyes to people in general, I feel like if people you live with every day can wake up in the morning and pretend like they love you. What would you think about people you meet outside of your circle? I have managed to keep my eyes and ears open toward people in general. Jesus said that in the last days because inequity has abounded, the love of many has waxed cold. Nobody in this day and hour has any respect for anybody. Nevertheless, life goes on and therefore I started a new chapter in my life. So, know a new chapter begins.

> *Behold, the hour cometh, yea, is now come, That you shall be scattered Every man to his own, and shall Leave me alone, and yet I am not alone, Because the Father is with me*
>
> *JOHN 16:32KJV*

> *These things I have spoken unto you, That in me you might have peace. In the world, ye shall have tribulation: However, be of good cheer; I have overcome the world.*
>
> *JOHN 16:33KJV*

CHAPTER-TWELVE-PART 2

———

BEING LIED ON, TALKED ABOUT, MISUSED, AND ABUSE BY THE ONE YOU LOVE MOST

Put not your trust in Princes, Nor is the son of man, In whom there is no help

PSALMS 146:3KJV

Being lied on, talked about misuse, And abuse, by the one you love The most

I have been in Holiness for forty-three years, and I have had so many ups and downs until I have lost count of them all, you come out of one trial and you go into another, before that was handled you have more coming in before that trial ends.

Once you come over into Holiness that is when the trouble starts. You have developed more enemies than you had before you came over on the Lord's side. I have struggled with family rejection, and then we struggle with rejection from the church, not only in the church but also the jealousy, you have to deal with on the job. By you being, saved, you are always treated much differently, from most people. I have learned how to deal with my enemies. The people that I love most, have lied to, talked about me, and tried to deceive me most of all. Most of all I did not expect to be lied to by the children I adopted. It was the most hurtful moment in my life to have to endure the pain and suffering of the lies and the deceit that they had committed against me, to get out of my home, because they did not want structure. A home without rules is not a home. When you have children in your home, doing whatever they want to do is not a good place to be. I had to constantly deal with the lies, disrespect, and the ungodly acts they committed in my home. Here I go back and forth to church, I have the greatest confidence in the people of God, and come to find out all those years I have been In Holiness, I couldn't find one church person who told the truth about things. They will lie on you talk about you scandalize your name over the highway, and have everybody looking at you as if you are a liar. I was astonished at what I had experienced; being in the Ministry all these years, the people I trusted most were the ones who had been in Holiness for many years. Come to find out, didn't none of them tell the truth? I kept asking God how can this be, how could you sit up in the church all these years and not tell the truth lying and stealing in the House of God? In addition, as I traveled around the country, it became more and more obvious because iniquity about the love of many has waxed cold. There is no love anywhere you turn. However, I refuse to allow the devil to have me sitting up in the house of God and not amend my ways. We all have sinned and have come short of God's glory. I realize that you will not have any friends in Holiness, because of what you stand for, and that is truth. I searched for many of years to find people that stood for what I stood for, and I could not find them. I'm at a point in life where I stopped looking because If I didn't find them back then, how in the world will I find them now, since everything has changed for the worse, and the love of many has waxed cold? I had so many lies told on me by church people, that it made me very depressed. I thought when I had been saved, I was truly a changed person, and I thought that everybody was like me. I got married to a man when I was nineteen years of age, and the family told me so many lies on me that it was not funny. I had to get away from them people and leave them alone. I told them until you get yourself corrected, and start telling the truth, I do not want to be bothered by people like you. Because I do not have room in my circle to put up with a liar, gossip, and a busybody. I am a firm believer that if you do not have anything to say nice about a person, you should not say anything at all. The in-laws would insult me right in my face and think that I was supposed to take their abuse and put up with their lies, their backbiting, and their misconception of me. I moved back to the Chicago area and I have not visited them in eight years. My patients have run short, I can no longer tolerate a person who is not truthful, and who is sneaky and very deceptive. That is a spirit, and that spirit has been controlling them since birth. Because the Bible says that children were born liars. However, the rod of correction would drive it far from them. You cannot teach old dog new tricks, if you get to live to be old and you are still lying and being deceptive, there is not much hope for you, because once you reach adulthood you are supposed to know better. The only hope for you is to repent and turn your life over to God so that he can clean you up from those things that are not right. Then you find grown people, who like to keep mess going, that is because of the immaturity, in which they have not matured into adulthood. In addition, many never mature, because most people do not like change. In addition, when you fight change, that is a bad sign in which, you are going in the wrong direction in life. I am a firm believer that your young days, determine your old age. In other words, what you put out, is what you get back. Your family is the most dangerous because that is blood. In addition, you do not expect blood to harm you in any way. However, they will, and will not repent after the damage they have willfully done, and the damage they have untruthfully caused. Your own family will put you through hell, and will never blink an eye, and they will never come back and apologize for the trouble they have willfully caused you. I have watched different people on my job, sit around looking and watching, and waiting to see, what kind of trap they can catch you in. I have been lied to, on in these jobs talked about, misused, and abused, but Jesus said in his word that we are more than a conqueror through Jesus Christ. You have to endure a lot while you are on this Highway Road of Holiness. You must press, as you have never pressed before, to stay on the road to Heaven. Only the righteous and the pure in heart shall reign with God. No unclean person shall dwell up there with God. All backbiter liars, haters of men, and haters of God Shall have their part in the Lake that burns with fire and brimstone. That is why we continue to pray and fast, and go into consecration before God So that we may continue to be refilled daily with the power from on high for us to be able to stay on the road of Holiness. When family turns against you, friends, and even the church, then you have to figure out where to go and to whom do I turn next. That is why the Lord tells us not to put our trust and confidence in any man woman, boy, or girl. We have to realize that once we come off the devil's territory, he no longer has a hold on us to walk and do the things that he tells us to do. We are on the Lord's side now, so that creates enemies between you and your family, and the ones that sitting up in church playing with God, and think that they are on their way to heaven anyhow, and have not stopped lying and stealing in the house of the Lord. Do not fool yourself with the devil that gets into people they can look at you and tell who you are, and you can look at them and tell who they are. The spirit of God knows the devil, and the devil knows when the true spirit is operating in you. Then he starts to pick fights with you. We have to realize, that the devil is mad, because we came off his turf, and know you are on God's territory. So therefore, he is going to do all he can to distract you from following God, but you must hold on, even when you have been lied to, talked about, misused, and abused by the ones you love the most. Once you come over on the Lord's side the devil is going to come after you with everything he got. He is on his job, and that is what he does best, so we must be on ours praying and fasting so that we can continue to do the right thing in this present world because what we do here on this earth will determine where we will spend eternity at, the choice is ours. Once the devil gets a person to lie against you, he made a fool out of that person to commit a crime against you, and the person the majority of the time doesn't even know the devil has used them until their eyes come open and then they are trying to figure out what Have I done. In addition, when the lies do not stand up, that is when the backbiting and the deception creep in. I have experienced on my job, being lied to, talked about and false rumors spread all over the company. The next thing you know the devil used one person to tell a lie against me and the lie took root. After the lie takes root, then the devil gets just about everybody in the company to turn against you. However, one thing that stands assured is that the Word of God will stand amid men and in God. God will defend its own. That's why he told us to pray for them that despitefully misuse you, and lie against us, because we know what God is capable of, and we know that he will defend us at all costs. I have seen people fall dead for lying against me and falsely accusing me of things that I did not commit. That is why we have to forgive them and walk away because we are going to pay for everything we have done in this life, whether it was good or whether it was evil. When people find out you are a liar, no one will ever trust you. Because you cannot be trusted in any kind of way. However. Every word that comes out of your mouth, people think you are lying. I never could figure out why grown people lie. Children lie, the bible says that children are born a liar, but the rod of correction will drive it far from them. If you have become an adult, and still lying, then when your parents tried to correct that, they were unsuccessful and correcting you about your behavior. Therefore, you take that foolishness into your adult life. In addition, cause all these problems for yourself. Then you start, a family, how are you going to teach the children not to lie and you could not be corrected about your lying? Known here we go; we reap what we have sown. In addition, know the children are lying, and you should be able to see yourself in those children, to not only correct them but also get yourself corrected. Truth will always prevail over lies; righteousness will prevail, over unrighteousness. I find that people who lie about small things will lie about big things, so therefore you can never trust a liar. Not only will you lie, but you will also steal and commit other ungodly acts. The greatest disappointment in life is when the family talks about you and lies against you, and you are so hurt by the lies and the gossip, you just have to separate yourself from those types of people, because they are not like you, and the Lord speaks to us about having fellowship with the unfruitful works of darkness. I think the second most deadly disappointing thing you can ever endure in life is when the church talks about you and spreads lies about you all up and down the highway. However, I have been lied to in the church, but I am still standing, and the church folk did not even have the dignity nor respect to come back and ask for forgiveness. They are still going to church as if they have not done a thing wrong. I am a firm believer that if you try to ask a person to forgive you, how do you know that they will if you never ask? However, the lies that were told against me in the church did not prevail. He told me to be still and know that I am God. I stood still and I saw the salvation of the lord. In addition, I found out that your worst enemies are those that are of your household.

As we travel down life path

We must count on God to act very fast.

For Jesus is the way the truth and the light

Trust in him to always keep us in the daylight

When darkness come, and it seems like

We have no guide, he is always there to provide.

For he have said that he will never leave us,

Neither will he forsake us, for his Word is true

In addition, he cannot lie. For God is not like man that he should like

Nor like he the son of man that he should repent.

For if he said it he shall perform it.

Only thing we have to do is believe in his Word.

CHAPTER TWELVE-PART 3

HURTING PEOPLE
HURT OTHER'S

Be careful with you words, once they are said, They can only be forgiven, and not forgotten. Words scar more than you think. The tongue has no bones, However, it is strong enough to break a heart.

Be careful to do what is right in the eyes of everyone. If it is possible, as far as it depends on you, Live at peace with everyone

ROMANS: 12:17 KJV

Let us therefore follow the things, which make for peace, In addition, things wherewith one may edify another.

ROMANS: 14:19 KJV

As I have traveled down life paths, I find that people are so evil, the delivery set out to hurt you, because hurting people hurts others. Some people have allowed themselves to be hurt so badly until they start turning the tables, and begin to hurt everybody that they meet. They succeeded in doing unto others, just as others, have done unto them. What a sad state of mind to be in. Wanting other people to suffer in the same manner in which you have suffered. You do not take vengeance out on other people that have not done anything to you. You should have kept yourself in a position to be able to discern between a person's intent. You know people currently do not know the difference between good and evil. They are full of game, deception, and deceit, and you have to be wise enough to be able to distinguish the difference between a person's motive and intent. You have people out there who have not grown up yet, and while they have not grown up, they end up hurting everybody they meet. You must learn to protect yourself against the tricks of the enemy, the devil does not care who he uses. That is why you must pray for them that despitefully misuse you. Moreover, we must pray for them, for they do not, do what they do. When Jesus was hanging on the cross the two thieves were hanging with him, one on the left, and the other on the right. However, the one that was on the right said unto him, for if thou be the son of God, save me and yourself, and the other said Lord forgive me and remember me when thou go into thy kingdom, and right then and there the Lord had forgiven that man sins while he was hanging on the cross. Lord replied unto him that this day thou should be with me in paradise. One of the disciples asked Jesus how many times we forgive our brother, Jesus answered and said seventy times seven, that is a whole lot of forgiving. I raised four adopted children, and they were so mean and angry with their biological parents for giving them away. Until whatever you did for them was never good enough. I tried to give my nephew back to his mother. However, she would not accept him. Therefore, he carried that pain and anger throughout his life. As of this day, he is still suffering behind his mother not wanting him. But there was nothing that I could do to make her take him, he is now four years old and he is still carrying the hurt and pain around with him he has hurt so many people that I can't figure out how can he sleep at night. He can't sleep at night because that is the reason why he drinks heavily, and smokes pot all day long, even tried selling it, and had to go on probation, hurting people hurt others. He became so disrespectful to me in my house, I showed him the door, so he got mad because I put him out, I told him what am I to do just let you abuse me in my home and I'm not supposed to say nothing to you. Your behavior is going to get you into a lot of trouble; he has been very disrespectful to women. However, he needs to realize that we were not the cause of his problem, so why take it out on the one who tried to help you? Therefore, he started going up and down the start cursing at me and laughing at me calling me names in front of the neighbors that lived on the block, so I walked away and left him in the hands of the Lord. He went into the Military, in the branch of the Navy, and was disrespectful to his sergeants, and the other officers, that had ruled over him. I warned him that his attitude and his disrespectful behavior were going to cost him everything in life one day. Out in the bar in Japan and started flirting with the sergeant's girl, the Sergeant beat him down and then they put him out of the Navy on a bad behavior discharge. This boy had a Letter of Recommendation to go anywhere in the world he wanted to go from President Bill Clinton. Who throws their life away like that? He raised his hands against me and I went to my car to get a baseball bat if my brother hadn't grabbed me, no telling what I would have done to him, I told him as long as he lived in this life, he could never speak to me again in this world. It has been sixteen years and I have not spoken to him since, he had a son who was four months old and took the baby to the hospital to be circumcised and took the baby back to his house and put the baby in his bed, and found the baby dead the next morning. He called me up and told me that the baby died, and I asked him a question, where was the baby sleeping when he found the baby dead, he replied that the baby was in his bed. Therefore, I asked him what the baby was doing in your bed, at that age. The baby should have been in his crib, and I asked him how do you know that you did not roll over on the baby and smother the baby because you had been drinking and smoking that pot. Hurting people hurt others. In addition, he knows the pain that he has put others through. Nevertheless, he recognizes the pain that he has been put in. Hurting people hurt others. You have to be wise enough to be able to recognize those types of people and stay as far away from them as possible because some people will go to their graves with the hurt and pain that they have been carrying around with them for years. Some will never get past it, and because you cannot get past your hurt, you never mature nor do you ever grow into adulthood. Your growth has been stunted so, therefore, you are stuck in a childhood state of mind, and the older you get the angrier you will become, unless you find Jesus somewhere in life that will forgive you of your sins, and will also help you forgive yourself, and others that have hurt you. In addition, in so doing you will find yourself with a peace of mind in life, so that you may be able to do the right thing in the world, and be able to lie down and sleep at night.

Through all the pain and the suffering we feel God will be there to help us heal. Through all the toils and tares God will deliver us from all the snares.

CHAPTER-TWELVE-PART 4

ABUSIVE PEOPLE, ABUSIVE OTHER'S

In addition, whatsoever ye do in word or deed,
Do all in the name of the Lord Jesus,
Giving thanks to God and the father by him.
Colossians 3:17 KJV

Now ye also put off all these
Anger, wrath, malice, blasphemy, filthy
Communication out of your mouth.
Colossians 3:8 KJV

Abusive People Abuses Others

As you can see how hurting people goes around hurting others just because of what they had to go through within their lifetime. Therefore, it is with a person with the same frame of mind of abusing others. As you have read in the chapter before this one Hurts, people hurt others, and so it is that abusive people abuse others. Because of the abuse that they had to go through, they have the same mentality to abuse others who have abused them. In addition, in my lifetime I have known people who weren't abused. Nevertheless, because of Where they came from, there is a thing that is called a generational curse. So sometimes, the abusiveness of a person comes down the bloodline. Where the mother and the father were abusive and so are the children. You, know that old saying, you are what you eat? Moreover, the apple does not fall far from the tree.

There are so many different available treatments, and there is counseling available too. In this day and time, we do not have to walk around in that condition. You don't have to be abusive to others because things have not gone your way in life, I haven't met a person yet in this present world, where everything went their way in life. You have to recognize that you have an abusive problem first, and then be strong enough to go and seek help. I find that the majority of people in the world today hate to admit that they have a problem. In addition, as long as they do not see that they have a problem, it can never be addressed. Moreover, as long as you do not address the abuse issue, it will never get resolved. In addition, your life will never get any better, because you have not got the issue addressed. An abusive person is not only abusive to others, but they are also, abusive to themselves. However, they are carrying around a lot of anger, and animosity, which needs to be addressed. In addition, when those issues aren't addressed, it will lead you to start abusing drugs, and alcohol. In addition, once you start abusing drugs and alcohol, then you become addicted. Moreover, here we go, we have more issues to deal with. In addition, with all that being said all those issues I have addressed, can lead to suicide.

In addition, know you see no reason for you to continue to live because you feel like you have nothing to live for. You find that everybody you meet into contact with ends up getting hurt because of you and your past. I grew up in a family where my father was very abusive. He jumped on my mother every night. He waited until he thought everybody was asleep. And then he would come home two o'clock in the morning and wake my mother up out of her sleep and make her sit on the couch, and jump on her all night and then he would wake us up and try to make us hit her. I refused and I told him that he must stop because what he was doing is Wrong and I will not do what you are asking me to do, and I did not. We were very small children at that time. We just stood there and cried; we could not do anything because we were too small to help her.

CHAPTER THIRTEEN

———

He That Will Live Godly in Christ Jesus, Must Suffer Persecution

Blessed are the poor in spirit:
For theirs is the kingdom of heaven.

Blessed are they that mourn:
For they shall be comforted.

Blessed are the meek:
For they shall inherit the earth

Blessed are they, which do hunger
In addition, thirst after righteousness:
For they shall be filled.

Blessed are the merciful:
For they shall obtain mercy.
Blessed are the pure in heart:
For they shall see God.

Blessed are the peacemakers:
For they shall be called the
Children of God.

Blessed are they, which are persecuted
For righteousness sake: for theirs
Is the kingdom of heaven?

Blessed are ye, when men shall revile you,
In addition, persecute you, and shall say all manner of evil
Against you falsely, for my sake.

Rejoice and be exceeding glad:
For great is your reward in heaven:
For so persecuted they the prophets
Which were before you.

MATTHEWS 5:3-12

HE THAT WILL LIVE GODLY IN CHRIST JESUS MUST SUFFER

I remember when I first was saved; it was a time of rejoicing for me. I was so full of joy and full of life. I knew that something had happened to me, but I was not in the full knowledge of what that was. Not only was I so full of life, but I had been reborn again, into a world that I knew nothing about. Everything had changed around me. Even though I had changed, the old things that I did before I was saved did not exist anymore. However, a new way of doing things started manifesting itself in me. However, one thing that I could not understand was that trouble started coming my way which I did not understand since I was saved. Nobody explained to me that not everything was going to be easy. Matter of fact when your eyes come open, you can see things, as they are, which you could not see before you were saved. It's, as you are in another dementia. Trials and tribulations started coming upon me which I did not understand before I was saved, and now that I had been born again, it was scary. Because I did not hear the word trial and tribulations until I was saved. Strange things started happening, and I became increasingly.

Frightened. I started murmuring and complaining, and I became depressed, at everything that came upon me. In addition, I thought that since I had been saved, things were going to get better. However, it did not at first. Things had become worse over a period.

I did not think that I would be able to stay in the church this past year. Things in my life had become so difficult until I told myself that I was not going to stay in church and be married to a man who was on drugs. In addition, he did anything and everything he could, to support himself and his friend habit. That included stealing from me, and besides he did not have any remorse for his behavior. In addition, it has been forty-three years since I have been in Holiness. As I look back, it was a long hard journey and a rough one. However, God bought me through. However, learning that one thing is that the world is going to hate you for how you are, and what you stand for. I have been lied to, talked about, misused abused, and misunderstood. Jesus has already forewarned us that if they hated him without a cause, they are going to hate you the same way. For if, they did it to the green tree, what do you think that they will do to a dry tree? Because Jesus was the chief cornerstone, and they rejected him, so we are going to be rejected in the same manner. I find one true thing, when you even mention the name of Jesus, demons start to unleash. As I looked back forty-three years ago, it was not hard for me to be saved. And it wasn't difficult for me to give up a lot of things, because I had just turned nineteen, and I had not been in the streets, as I looked back forty- three years ago, it wasn't hard for me to get saved. In addition, it was not difficult for me to give up many things because I had not developed many unhealthy habits. In today's society, people are being saved today, and going back out into the world tomorrow. We know that we are in the last days, and the prophecy of Jesus Christ is being fulfilled. I had so many obstacles in my way, and at times, I did not see my way out. Each day I had to fight like I depended upon it. When you are living with someone who is working against you that is the most difficult task I ever had to endure, in these forty-three years of Holiness. I felt like my soul was at stake here. He did not want to be saved, so he did not want me to be saved. However, the power of God did prevail. Everything I tried to accomplish, he fought against me. However, everything I bought and tried to have, he stole it. To have an enemy living in the home with you is a dangerous task. You cannot sleep. You are up all night long watching and waiting for the enemy's next move. However, he thought that he was so slick and smooth he could get away with everything. However, the power of God prevailed in the end. You can only stay in a trial for so long, and then there has to be a change made. Therefore, after being in that trial for a few years, I decided to go my own way. However, a house is not a home when you do not have any peace within that house. I do not advise anybody to live with someone you know it is not going to work. I tried but I could not put up with the drama any longer. That is what happens when you marry a person who is immature and has not grown up yet. They do things as a child to keep you aggravated all the time. In addition, it is one mischievous thing after another, to get the attention that the parents were not able to give them. I did not sign up to marry somebody's kid and to try to help raise him. I made a vow to God forty-three years ago. I promised God I would work for him, and I would hold out until my change came. It is hard to turn a person around especially when they have come down through hard trials and tribulations, and God has been right by their side every step of the way. The devil will come through your wife, your kids, and your family. He will use people on your job, and in the church, but you have to be determined that you will not let nothing and nobody separate you from the love of God. For forty-three years I was persistent, to let nothing separate me from God's love. I came down through hard trials and tribulations, through blood sweat, and tears, to be able to go forth under the anointing, and in the power of the highest God. Once you learn the power of prayer, and what God can do, when you call on his great name, that makes you more determined to keep on serving the Lord in the beauty of Holiness. I am pressing toward the mark of a higher calling Of God. I know that it is not easy, but if you put on your armor and keep yourself protected from your head to your feet, and front and back cover, with praying and fasting, you will come out a winner. The first half of my journey is completed; however, I am starting the second half. I started in the ministry at the age of twenty-one, and I started the Evangelist field at the age of twenty-three. I have been in Ministry for forty-one years, and I have been an Evangelist on the field for thirty-nine years. I just want you to know I am not tired yet. I have only completed half of my journey. Know twenty-twenty-one starts a new chapter of my journey. Getting ready to come off the Evangelist field, and know the office of a Pastor starts a new chapter in my life. However, the first half was so tough, some days I did not see how I could make it through some of the storms I had to go through. The second half of the journey is going to be worse than the first half. After all that I have been through, and I saw how God brought me through every trial and tribulation in the first half, I am willing and ready. Through the knowledge and the wisdom of God, he will teach you how to be an overcomer. On this highway of Holiness, either you will do or die, or I refuse to die because I am trying to make heaven my home, so, therefore, I must stay in the race. The race is not given to the swift, nor the battle given to the strong, but is given to the one that endures to the end. You must run to the end, to receive the prize. Unless you are crowned lawfully, you cannot win the race. However, he that will live Godly in Christ Jesus must suffer persecution. I do not expect to do great work for the Lord, and not be persecuted. That goes for everybody, if you are going to do something meaningful in this world, and leave a mark behind in the world, you have to prepare yourself to go through hard trials and tribulations, and then go through with joy. I remember when some of the apostles, when some were thrown into prison, and others were beaten, they did not complain, they started rejoicing, giving God Glory, because they were glad that God had found them worthy to be able to suffer for his namesake. They kicked me out of every church I went to. The devil knows the true saints of God, and when you are trying to deceive people, the devil knows how you are. However, he that will live Godly in Christ Jesus must suffer persecution. For if, we do not arm ourselves to suffer for the name of the Lord Jesus, we will not reign with him. At all costs, we must do everything in our power to maintain our position in God. As we engage in spiritual warfare, we realize that we are not wrestling against flesh and blood, but against principalities, against powers, against the rulers of the darkness of this world, against spiritual wickedness in high places.

EPHESIANS 6:12 KJV

There are only two types of spirits in this world. You have the spirit of good, which produces righteousness, and then you have the spirit of evil, which produces unrighteousness. Therefore, you must be able to discern which spirit you have. Either you walk in righteousness, or you walk in unrighteousness, therefore you determine for yourself, which spirit is going to control you. We have choices in this world, and I advise you that you must choose wisely. This is why prayer and consecration, are always needed, because both spirits, are always present within us. Those two spirits of good and evil are always in a war within us daily. However, the only thing we have down on the inside of us, to be able to win the battle between good and evil, is the Holy Spirit. That is the only thing that can conquer evil. He that will live Godly in Christ Jesus must suffer persecution. When we desire to do good, evil is always present. That is why we walk with God so that we can always try to do what is right in the sight of God and man. The evil spirit that is lurking in the earth is gaining strength. Because the devil knows that, his time is limited. In addition, he is trying to get as many souls as he possibly can to lose their souls, just as he lost his. We all know the difference between right and wrong, good and evil. In addition, we are going to have to give an account of what we do know. Whether we want to accept it or not God is real, and the devil is too. Satan used to be the director of the choir in heaven until he got jealous of God and his Glory, then God kicked him out of heaven, and Satan took a third of the angels with him. When God kicked him out of heaven, he fell like lightning. That is what happens when you set a plot against someone, usually it backfires.

Moreover, he said unto them, I beheld Satan as lightning fall from heaven.

LUKE 10:18 KJV

Just think about that scripture, you cannot hardly see lightning, so therefore we could not even get a glimpse of him falling. Satan is going to use whosoever he will, and when he finishes using you to do the wrong things in life, he will run off and leave you, all by yourself. Moreover, in the end, the only one you will have to help you is God. The Lord has told us that he will never leave you nor forsake you. You must choose wisely because you do not have many chances to do the right thing in life. I have seen people in their teenage years, going into adulthood, make the wrong choice, and end up in the streets, until they got old. After being on drugs and alcohol for over forty years, they decide they are tired and it is time to come to the Lord. Bad choice, wrong move. Disobedience will cost you everything. He that will live Godly in Christ Jesus will suffer persecution. This is the reason we strive to stay with the Lord. However, it is not easy, but we must be persistent, to stay in the race. Yes, we are persecuted, and we are lied to and talked about, but we have a much bigger goal in the making. This thing will happen to you once you have a mind to serve the Lord. There is nothing easy in serving the Lord, simply because we are in a race, and we are striving to win the crown, to win the crown, you must walk in righteousness. Living an unrighteous life, will not get you the crown. You must reject evil, to stay in the race. We must keep the faith, and stand on what we believe in. I can recall early one morning, I heard the voice of the Lord speak to me, and he said that I was going to be hated, by all men for his namesake. I did not fully comprehend it at first, but down the road, everywhere I went, on the job, in the church, in the family, I was, hated for the name of Jesus. It took me a long time to get used to that. I had become very depressed about the rejection that I had to go through. It has been going on for years in my life. Hated and rejected by family, church members, and coworkers. By everybody, I meet. I have not found a truth in this world yet. People will laugh and grin in your face, and turn right around and tell a lie on you, in your face. Family will talk about you, and lie on you as well. I remember the song that says; there is not a friend, like the lowly Jesus, no not one. I found one friend who has been dear to me; he has stood by my side and has never left me yet. On this road to glory, you must stay in obedience to God. In addition, every time God would send me somewhere, or send me to someone to give them a message, there have been repercussions behind the obedience to God. I was thrown out of every place I went.

The persecution began to get a little bit easier, down the road. The people you have confidence in are the ones that do the most damage to you. This is why the Scripture tells us not to put our trust in any man. I am learning how to keep my mouth closed when the enemy is in authority.

I have been in Holiness for forty-three years, and it does not get any easier. The more you depart from sin, the worse the devil will use people to come after you. In addition, he sends people after you, because he wants you to give up, turn around, go back out in the world, and do what everybody else does. However, you have to be strong and very courageous, to complete the assignment that God has entrusted to you. Through hard trials and tribulations, we must learn to trust God every step of the way. Jesus came and showed us the way, and he paid that price for us to be an overcomer. In addition, after he went away, he told us that he was going to send us help, after he left, and return unto his father. He sent back the Holy Spirit to lead us and guide us into the knowledge of all truth and righteousness. When the spirit leads us, we live by the spirit, and when we live by the spirit, we should not live in sin. Jesus came down to redeem us back to the Father, and he came and told us the truth, because he spoke truth into power, they sought to kill him. They persecuted him because he said he came in the name of the Father, and they killed him for telling the truth. They seek to do the same thing to us for telling the truth, but we have to stand just as the Apostles have stood. Jesus sent back the comforter for us to have the same power to be able to overcome, just as he overcame. We cannot overcome obstacles that come upon us without the power. However, without the power, you cannot live free from sin. Jesus told Nicodemus you must be born again, and Nicodemus asked Jesus, how can a man be born when he is old, can he enter into his mother's womb a second time. Jesus replied and said to Nicodemus, you must be born of the water and the spirit, or you cannot even see the Kingdom of God. Jesus was sent to this earth to redeem us back to the Father. In addition, it is our choice if we want to accept the Lord as our Savior. I do advise you to choose wisely, however, it is your decision. In addition, whatever decision you make, you own it. Once, it is appointed unto a man to die, and after death comes the judgment. Jesus was the Lamb that was slain from the foundation of the world. Moreover, he was slain for the sins of many. For whosoever will let him come, eat and drink without money. If life was a thing that money could buy, the rich man would live, and the poor man would have to die. This is why we will not let our religion die.

For I know that in me, (that is, in my flesh,) dwells no good thing: for to will is present with me; but how to perform that which is good I find not.

ROMANS 7:18 KJV

For the good that I would I do not: but the evil, which I would not, that I do.

ROMANS 7:19 KJV

Now if I do that I would not, it is no more I that do it, but sin that dwells in me.

ROMANS 7:20 KJV

I find then a Law, that, when I would do good, evil is present with me.

ROMANS 7:21 KJV

This is the reason we fast and pray so that we do not live after the flesh. To live after the flesh, will cause you to die a spiritual death. Nevertheless, to live after the spirit will cause you to have life everlasting. When you live after the flesh you will do just about anything, you want to do, and you will not have any repentance behind the things you do and speak. We live for God because we do not want to live in sin; the Holy Spirit helps us to live right. There is no good thing that the Lord will withhold from us if we walk upright. When we are persecuted, and worry starts to set in, that is because unbelief is trying to take over. We must stand firm, keep our heads up, and look unto God from which comes our help because help is coming.

Trials and tribulations happen all the time, whether saved or unsaved. You are going to have to go through something all the time as long as you live on this earth. We are saved; we know how to pray and turn it over to the Lord. That makes it much easier for us not to have to carry the burden because God is our burden carrier and our burden barrier.

As I pray day by day
I ask the Lord who is always there to
make a way
As I strive up the mountain side God is
working on my pride.
Teach me how to stay in your will.
Lord, I will do my best
And learn how to stand still.

CHAPTER-THIRTEEN-PART 2

THE BATTLE IS NOT GIVEN TO THE SWIFT NEITHER TO THE STRONG BUT IT IS GIVEN TO THE ONE THAT ENDURETH TO THE END

No man put a gun to our head and made us sign up to get into this race. This is not an ordinary race, but this is a race for the battle of our souls. In an ordinary race, you have to register to participate. No registration, no participation. In an ordinary registration, you will receive a number, while running in the race, that you might be identified. They do not call out a winner by name, they call you out by the number, you received during your registration. The first one who crosses the finish line wins the top prize, in an ordinary race. In addition, the race that we have signed up for is spiritual. We are running for our lives and the saving of our souls. While they are seeking a corruptible crown, we are seeking an incorruptible crown. You do not get your reward until you have finished the race. In other words, you are not crowned lawfully until you cross the finish line. We as the people of God are working for a crown of eternal life. However, we must complete the assignment that God has given to us in this present life. We have been given a task to do by God, and we must find ourselves doing it, to the best of our ability. The race is not to the swift, nor the battle to the strongest, but it is to the one that runs to the end. In God's race, there are more than a few winners. Although there will be many winners, we will not all receive the same prize. However, to receive your prize, you must finish the race strong.

One thing about God he is not going to give us a corruptible reward, our reward is incorruptible. He has promised to give us a crown of eternal life if we finish strong. Everybody who signed up to run in the race has agreed to the same pay. No matter when you signed up, to get in the race, you agreed to accept the same pay as the one that signed up before you, and the one that have signed up after you. However, there will be no misunderstanding with God. His word still stands, when everything around you fail, there is no failure in him. One thing about being in this race, we can all run at our own pace which is why the race is not too swift. No matter how fast we run, we will not be awarded for being the fastest runner, while striving for an incorruptible crown. We will be awarded for staying, in the race and making it to the finish line. There are many trials and tribulations on the road to Glory; we must fight until we cannot fight any longer. So many obstacles come up in our way, while we are running in this race. Many sleepless nights, and so many tears we have to shed, nevertheless we must stay in the race, no matter how hard it gets, and how complicated it may seem, stay in the race. We must continue on our knees in prayer, and consecration, to be able to stay in the race. Prayer fasting, and the Word of God are our weapons, to defend ourselves, while we are running in this race. There are many afflictions of the righteous, but the Lord will deliver us out of them all. As we continually fight our way to the finish line, we must keep the faith, however, without faith it is impossible to reach the finish line. Nobody told us that this race was going to be easy, but we did not expect it to be that hard either. For we are more than conquerors, through him that loved us. We fight until we cannot fight anymore. And, when the battle gets too strong, God will step in and send his angles to deliver us out of every situation that we can't see our way out of. From 2002 until 2014, I went through a trial that I thought would take me out. The enemy tried everything in his power to stop me. It was one trial after another, I found myself in a very dark depressed state of mind, and I did not know how I was going to come out of it dead or alive. I had so many sleepless nights; however, I had to go see a doctor for insomnia and post- traumatic stress disorder. However, the medication did not even help. I had everything, and everybody, to come against me, just because of whom I represented, and that is Christ. It was not me people hated; it was the Christ that lived down on the inside of me. Oh, but one day, I laid down on my living room sofa, and I fell asleep, and Jesus appeared unto me, I looked up he was standing between heaven and the earth, and his hands were folded in front of him. I looked up and he looked down at me and he started smiling, and I spoke and said Jesus that is you, and he said unto me, my friend, grab hold. I had people chasing me trying to harm me, and the people that were behind me were people that I knew, some were family members, and others were church people. His wings came from behind him, into a praying hand, and as I went to take both of my hands, to grab hold of Jesus' wings, before I could touch his wings his power lifted me out of the midst of my enemies and sat me down into a place of safety, and he disappeared. Then he appeared two more times and did the same thing, and he disappeared again. I looked around and my enemies were coming after me again, and I called on the Lord, and I heard his voice from heaven, he said I came down three times, and I am not coming down again, he then put a gun in my hands that had a barrel bigger than my hands. In addition, he replied unto me, you see what I have put in your hands, I answered yes Lord, and he then said I want you to use what I just put in your hand. He told me that he was not coming down again. I turned around and my enemies were upon me. I told them to open up their mouth, I put the barrel of the gun inside their mouth and I pulled the trigger, and white smoke came out of it, and they disappeared. I put the barrel of the gun in everyone's mouth that was in my midst, and after pulling the trigger they all disappeared.

However, after I had that vision, people started falling dead around me. One thing that I know about God you do not mess with one of his little children, because he will punish you for it. The battle is not ours; it belongs to the Lord. Afterward, I was able to get back up and, dust myself off, and get back in the race. I stumbled and fell while running.

However, God was there to help me get back up and start running again. It looks like every two or three years I have to go through a storm, and that storm lasts three years at the most. Even when Jesus appeared unto me, and put that gun in my hands, for me to be able to deal with my enemies, I was reminded of Jesus when he went to the cross and rose again on that third day, he told the disciples that all power had been given unto him. Therefore, he rose again and endowed us with that same power. However, he told the disciples that greater works than what he did, they were going to do because he was going unto his father. Jesus has given us the power to run this race. We must learn how to use the power he has given us, to be able to stay in the race. We are in a battle for our very lives, and we must learn how to use the tools that he has put in our hands. Those tools are our weapons, and we must use our weapons to be able to stay in the race. For the scripture has told us that we fight not against flesh and blood, but against principalities, and powers, against the rulers of darkness, and spiritual wickedness in high places. We cannot conquer wickedness with physical warfare. You can only conquer wickedness through spiritual warfare. We must stay in the race, and learn how to finish strong. Giving our life over to the Lord is just the start of our journey. I was saved at the age of nineteen, at the age of twenty-one I, was called to the ministry, and at the age of twenty-three, I started the Evangelist field. The Lord moved me fast. As I began to step out on faith at the age of twenty-three, trouble got worse than it was from the beginning. However, I did not let that stop me, and cause me to get out of the race. Many times, I wanted to give up, but when I thought about it, I said to myself where can I go, and who can I turn to? Forty-three years ago, I registered with God to get in the race, not knowing what I had signed up for. I was in for a rude awakening. I learned fast that this was going to be a battle for my soul. Knowing that my soul was in jeopardy of dying and going to hell. I had to spend a lot of time in prayer and fasting, seeking God's Face to be able to stay in the race. It was a challenge of a lifetime.

In my forty-three years in Holiness, I have seen many come and go. I have seen people get in the race, and figure out that it was too hard for them and get right back out. However, after they left the race, the most terrible thing in the world happened to them, some did not live long after they left the race. I, have seen some lose their mind and was never able to recover to get it back. The journey does get hard, and unbearable, but I learned to stand still and wait upon the Lord. I have had some good days and some bad days, but all of my good days outweigh my bad days. I will not give up, I will not give in, and I cannot turn back. I must stay in the race because we are almost at the finish line, the end is near, and we must fight on until the race is finished. Knowing this one thing that one day if we do not die in the faith, we are subject to be slain for our faith in Our Lord and Savior Jesus Christ. So, we must be prepared to give up all for the Lord Jesus to obtain the crown.

> *In addition, this I do for the Gospel's sake,*
> *That I might be partaker thereof with you.*

> *Know you not that they, which run in a race, run all,*
> *However, one received the prize*
> *So run, that ye may obtain.*

> *And every man who strives for the*
> *Mastery is temperate in all things.*

> *Now they do it to obtain a corruptible crown.*
> *But we can be incorruptible.*

> *I therefore so run,*
> *Not as uncertainly; so, fight I,*
> *Not as one, that better the air.*

*Nevertheless, I keep under my body, and bring it into
subjection: Lest that by any means,*

*When I have preached to others,
I should be a castaway.*

1 CORINTHIANS 10:23-27 KJV

*AS I WALK THIS ROAD TO GLORY LORD HOLD
MY HAND AND KEEP ME HOLY.
UNTO THE O'LORD DO I PUT MY TRUST
NEVER LET ME BE PUT TO SHAME*

CHAPTER-THIRTEEN-PART 3

———

When you have done all, you can do
To stand. Stand ye therefore anyhow.
And fight the good fight of faith Laying hold on eternal life.

Finally, my brethren,
Be strong in the Lord, and the power of his might.

Put on the whole armor of God,
that ye may be able to stand against the wiles of the devil.

For we wrestle not against
Flesh and blood, but against principalities,
Against powers, against the rulers
Of the darkness of this world,
Against spiritual wickedness in high places.

Wherefore take unto you the whole.

Armor of God that ye may be able to withstand in the
evil day, and having done all to stand.

Stand, therefore, having your lions
Girt about with truth,
And having on the breastplate of righteousness.

And your feet shod with the
Preparation of the Gospel Of peace.

Above all, taking the shield of faith,
Wherewith ye shall be able
To quench all the fiery darts of the wicked.

> *Moreover, take the helmet of salvation,*
> *And the sword of the spirit*
> *Which is the Word of God.*
>
> *Praying always with all prayer,*
> *And supplication in the spirit,*
> *And watching thereunto,*
> *With all perseverance and*
> *Supplication for all saints.*

EPHESIANS 6:10 – 18 KJV.

As, we continue in the race we must fight the good fight of faith. After we have done all to stand, we must continue to keep on standing. This is a hard journey, it is a lonely journey, but one thing we do know is that we have a friend in Jesus. Moreover, there is not a friend like the lowly Jesus, no not one. As we continue to stand, in the Lord having done all to stand, we must take hold of the shield of faith. Without faith, it is impossible to please God. You cannot go anywhere if you do not have faith. You will not be able to get through half of the journey without faith. Because faith is what is going to see you through to the end. As I told you earlier in the chapter, you must stay in the race. To stay in the race and win the prize you must have faith. The only way you can stand is by faith. For God has promised not to leave us nor forsake us. That is all the assurance we need to be able to stand. In every situation, you must turn everything over to God and trust, that he will fix everything. Forty-three years in Holiness, I have not seen him leave one situation undone yet. He may not have come when I wanted him to come, but he was never late. He showed up and he showed out. In addition, in most cases he over did himself. He done more than what I expected him to do. After you have, done all you can do to stand, stand ye therefore anyhow. Even when you cannot see your way, stand still and see the salvation of the Lord. He will show up and fight for you. I am remembering when my trials had got so hard, and I could not see my way out, I laid down and fell into a deep sleep. In addition, there were an angel in front of me, two on the side and one in the back. The one that was leading me through had a sword, the two that held me up on each side had a sword, and the one that was in the rear had a sword. The road had become dangerous, so God had to send me help in order to be able to make it off that dangerous path. The angels were equipped, and they were armed and dangerous. They saw me through safely. This is why it is so important to fast and pray, because we do not know where danger lies. Through prayer and fasting, it keeps us alert of the danger, and of all the fiery darts, that the enemy throws against you. That is why the Lord told us to take up the shield of faith so that we may be able to quench all the fiery darts of the wicked. In other words, with faith in God we can block all the tricks of the enemy. When you have, done all you can do to stand, hold fast to that which is good. In addition, having you lions girt about with the truth. You must tell people the truth no matter how hard it is to tell them. The truth sometimes hurts us all. Nevertheless, we must not live unto the Lord a lie. As we preach the truth to others, we must live by the same word as they do. However, righteousness exalts a nation, but sin is a reproach unto any people. You must have on the breastplate of righteousness on. When men see your good works, they want to follow God just like you. I have had so many people desiring to be like me. I told many of them to be like me is to give up your life completely. Not many people want to give up their life style, in order to live a Holy and a righteous life. It is not an easy thing to do. I was so fortunately, because, I came to God at the age of nine-teen, so therefore I did not have anything to give up at that early age. In addition, we should train up a child in the way he should go, when he grows old, he shall not depart from the teaching you have taught him. We have to be strong in the Lord, because the devil will have himself a field day with you, if you show signs of weakness. The devil will try you to the end, so therefore you must fight to the end. When you begin to worry and not have no peace behind the things that you have to endure, you do not have the faith. Because faith causes you to have perfect peace in God. In addition, no faith causes you to worry, about the things you are going through. However, your feet must be shod with the preparation of the Gospel peace. God word is so important. David said that the word is a light unto my feet and a lamp unto my path. Therefore, you should always have your shoes on. However, always be ready for instructions at all times. God word will lead us and guide us down this dark and dangerous path. For his word is a light unto my feet, if I follow the light, I cannot stray off the path. For it is a very dangerous thing to stray away from the path, in which the Lord is guiding you down. There is danger on the path; in addition, there is also danger off the path. However, if you stay on the path, you are guaranteed that help is coming if you run into danger. If you decide to stray off the path, there is no guarantee that help is on the way, because you have strayed away from the truth, and when you walk away from the truth. You are no longer under protection in the blood. Stay on the road, because there is peace, safety, joy, and happiness on the highway of Holiness. David said Thy Word Lord have I hid in my heart that I might not sin against thee. We read and meditate on God word daily, so that we may be able to stay on the right path. Without God Word the world is lost, and we would be lost too, if we do not continue in his word. I have seen many people go to church for years and still do not understand the bible. That is rather shocking, because what are you doing sitting in church all those years for? Your heart has to open up, in order to be able, receive what the spirit has to say to the church. However, the church is you. If God word is not in your heart, how can you be led and guided by the spirit of the living God. You have nothing down on the inside to tell you the difference between right and wrong, so therefore you will continue to go in your own way all the days of your life. It is not as if God has not tried to turn you around, and put you on the right path, it just that you will not listen. In addition, when you have been going in your own way for so many years, afterwards God will eventually walk away and leave you alone. You area as the horse, in which bits has to be put in his mouth to be controlled. David said the Lord is a light unto my feet, and a lamp unto my path, so therefore I cannot walk in error. Stay on the road, and fight the good fight of faith laying hold on eternal life. I do not know about you; I am not over here playing around; it is too late in the day to be fooling around with your soul. I have been toiling a long time, it is not time for me to throw in the towel, the night is far spent, and the day of the Lord is at hand. He is on his way back to take vengeance on all that would live ungodly. His word does not lie, he came as our Lord and savior, and he will return as our Judge. For he said in his word that the saints will judge the world. You will not have any excuse for why you did not believe his word. For he sent his Word to heal deliver and to set us free. God is not going to make anyone do anything they do not want to do. It is your choice, and your free will. However, woe be unto to him if he preaches not the Gospel. Your choice, your own free will, you decide.

After this I looked, and behold
A door was opened in heaven:

And the first voice which
I heard was as it were of a trumpet
Talking to me; which said,
Come up hither, and I will
Show thee things, which must
Be hereafter.

And immediately I was in the
Spirit And, behold, a throne
Was set in heaven, and one
Sat on the throne.

And he that sat was to look upon
Like a Jasper and a Sardine stone.

And there was a rainbow round
About the throne, in sight Like unto an Emerald.

And round about the throne,
Were four and twenty seats:
And upon the seats I saw four and twenty elders
Sitting clothed in white raiment;
And they had on their heads
Crowns of gold.

And out of the throne proceeded
Lightnings and thundering
And voices: and there were seven
Lamps of the fire burning
Before the throne, which are the
Seven spirits of God.

And before the throne
There was a sea of glass like
Unto crystal: and in the
Midst of the throne, and
Round about the throne, were four
Beast full of eyes, before|
And behind him.
REVELATION 4:1-6 KJV

And I saw in the right hand
Of him that sat on thethrone
A book written within
And on the backside,
Sealed with seven seals.

And I saw a strong angel
Proclaiming with a loud voice,
Who is worthy to open the book,
and to lose the seals thereof?

And no man in heaven,
Nor in earth. Neither

Under the earth was able
To open the book, neither to
Look thereon.

And I wept much, because
No man was found worthy to open
and read the book
Neither to look thereon.

REVELATIONS 5:1-4 KJV

BEHOLD THE LAMB OF GOD
THAT TAKETH AWAY THE SINS OF THE WORLD.

CLOSING

2ND CHRONICLES 20: 13-17

After growing up into a family of thirteen children, and raised by a single mother with no help, I did not really see life as being difficult. Maybe I paid no thought to it, because I already had dreams of what I wanted to do. When I got into the sixth grade, I wanted to be a secretary. Therefore, when I got to middle school, typewriters had become a course, so I took my first typing course, and I had done well in the course. So, I became fascinating with machines. Therefore, when I began high school, data entry came out, so I took a course in keypunching, and I succeeded in that course. Afterwards computers came out. The, I dropped out of high school because of problems with my mom. Went to Job Corp, end up being put out of there. Met my first husband in Job Corp, and ended up moving to Chicago at the age of nineteen. As I arrived there, I went back to school, and got my GED and started college at the same time. Therefore, I majored in Computer science, with a GPA 3.79. In addition, afterward I started Computer learning center, to learn how to operate the hardware and the software. I graduated from the computer school, but I still had to further my education. After being saved at the age of nineteen, and being in the Ministry know for forty-one years, traveling around the country for thirty-nine years of those years. On down the road I started Wright-State University, to Major in Political Science, and I thought about that field, then I told myself no, because you have to be a liar and a cheat to be in politics. Therefore, I change my major to Real Estate and Appraisals. In addition, I took courses in Business

Law. Enrolled in Sinclair Community College for Real Estate and Appraisals. Completed another course in Real Estate Appraisals at Swic Community College.

In all the hours I have accumulated, I am transferring them over to accounting to get my Bachelors. In the course of my journey, I have raised four adopted children; two of them were family members, and the other two were out of the child welfare system.

Because you grow up poor, does not mean you have to allow yourself, to get to be an adult, and continue down that path of poverty. We growing up in a small town, we did not know what poverty was. However, we had food on the table, we never evicted, lights, gas, phone, and water were never were shut off during the years we were kids. My mother always preached to us, never go out and have all those kids the way I did. We had a choice back in the day either go to school, or end up on welfare and food stamps. By growing up with thirteen children in your household, there was no way I was going down that path. It was very hard trying to help raise some of those children. Especially the younger ones that was up under us. They were hardheaded and contrary. There was no way I was going to put up with that when I became an adult. Even though I started on the wrong track, I did not end up on the wrong track. When I left home at the age of nine-teen, I Immediately went straight back to school, to get education and a job. This has been an incredible journey for me. I would not take nothing for the experience I had to go through, because it taught me a lesson of a lifetime. Especially after being in Ministry at an early age. It has been a hard journey, but a rewarding journey. February twenty-third 2021, will be forty-three years in Holiness. When I started out, however I did not think I would make it five years in the church. In addition, coming from a family of thirteen children. It was just so amazing to me that we never went hunger. I have met people with two or three children, and could not provide a stable home, and food to go on the table for them. I gave my mother an A plus for a job well done. She labored and done her best, most women would have put all those children in foster care, and ran off and left them all. However, she stayed right there, even when my father ran off and left all of us, after attempting to kill her, and cutting her up nine hundred and eighty-nine stitches with a razor, and leaving her for dead. However, to God be the Glory she lived to see all of us get grown. She always preached to us go to school and get and education, and try to get the things you want that I was not able to give you. We never complained. We were not hungry, we had clean clothes, and we did not care about material things. When we reach the age of eighteen, we then start making our own decisions. Whatever, choices you make starting out on your journey, those are the choices you will have to live with. Make sure you make the right choices so that you will not have any regrets. Because some choices cannot be overturned, you will have to live with certain choices for the rest of your life. I can remember when I was about sixteen years old, I would always be daydreaming about my future, and what my house was going to look like. I had big ideas about my education. I would dream about having nice cars, and traveling around the world. I am a firm believer when you reach the age between sixteen and seventeen, you should already know which direction you want to go, and what you want to do with your life when you get grown. When you have been bought up in the right manner, these things automatic comes into play. Your mind will automatic be set into play on what to do before you graduate from high school. I have seen so many kids finish high school, and just starts bumming around until they end up being caught up with the wrong crowd, and end up on drugs, or either in prison. There was no sense of direction, on which way to go. Whoever, some had the training, but decides to do what they want to do, and go their own way, which led them down a path of no return for some of them. In addition, most have that do not care attitude, as to where they do not care about anything or anybody. Some end up dead or in prison, I have seen some ends up shot up, and some end up paralyzed for the rest of their life. What future is there for you after all these things take place? If you live through all these bad mishaps, you will have a long time to think about what you should have done when you were told. These consequences take place when you disobey instructions. I am a firm believer that parents should monitor their children's friends. Because children that is not properly supervised, should not be hanging with your children. They are a bad influence on your children, and people will see your child, as being one of the birds that is flocking together. Unfortunately, we have a huge number of teenagers that has been left unattended, to care for themselves. That is the main cause of our young people being addicted to drugs and alcohol. In addition, that is why many young women and men start out into prostitution. Many have joined gangs, start selling drugs, because they do not see hope. Furthermore, they do not feel like anybody care about them because of their upbringing, and they end up turning to the streets and to gangs. I hope this book find s many that is caught up into situations, that they feel like they can't get out of hopeful, and encouraging for you to look up, and allow God to pick you up, because he can and he will if you let him. I started out feeling as if nobody loved me. I did not feel the reel love from my parents, because she had her favorites. Nevertheless, I left home, and because I got in the church at the age of nineteen, it saved my life. Being in church and knowing God gave me a different outlook on life. It is a hard situation, having a life on the streets without God and education. It is also a form of suicide, being out their alone. I am writing this book to inspire as many people as I possibly can old and young. To let you know that there is nothing too hard for God. If he did it for me, he will do the same for you. If he blessed me, he will bless you. For there is a reality in serving a true and a living God. I felt so alone for so many years; however, I turned to the church, for support as I began to mature. However, I was under the influence of older people that counseled me along my journey. However, one thing I have to say is that you must be willing to listen, and accept responsibilities for your actions. Made a few mistakes as a teenager, but corrected them, as I became an adult. I took heed to instructions, and words of wisdom. I put common sense into practice, and I made it work for me. And we that made it through our teenage years over into adult hood, going into our old age have a responsibility to reach out and grab others in, the same way someone grabbed us in, and saved our life. I got married too young, at the age of nineteen, and I became very depressed, however it was not the kind of relationship I had hoped for. It was so depressing to see a young man strung out on drugs and alcohol, especially after having a grandmother that was an ordained Minister.

There are many tears, and pain and suffering on this highway. This is a hard race, and a tough race. However, remember one thing, the race is not given to the swift neither the battle to the strong, but it is given to the one that endure to the end. You must stay on the path in order to finish the race. Stay the course, in order to stay with God. There are going to be many of times you are going to be knocked down, by the trials and tribulation of this world. Nevertheless, you must pick yourself up by your bootstraps, and dust yourself off and get back in the race. Once you are back up continuing to pray and fast, so that God will wipe away the tears of pain and sorrow that you are going through. We must complete the task God has set before us. By not completing the task, we are going to be held countable for the work not being completed. If you stay down, when you fall, that means you have given up. In addition, giving up in Christ is not an option. Christ did not give up as they were dragging him from judgement hall to judgement hall. In addition, the after all that, he yet went on and completed the missing his father had assigned for him to do. He went on to the cross and gave up his life for as many as would believe on his name. Do not make the choice to give up and get out of the race. If you make the choice to give up, however you have made a decision to go back into the world, and the trials and tribulations would be much harder than they were before you came in out of the world. However, Satan is mad because you left him the first time, and know God is upset because you left him and went back out into the world to serve Satan again. You have a problem either which way you go. Please make wise decisions, because in the end it will pay off. There will be rewards in the end, when the race is finished. However, the battle is won to those that endure to the end.

When you have done all, you can do to stand, you need to stand anyhow. We get tired, and we get weak while running in this race. In addition, when it seems like the cares of this life have taken a hold on us, we must give it over to the Lord and allow God to carry our burdens. Sometimes these burdens get too hard to bear. You give up and you give in because you do not know how to turn situations over to God and allow him to fix it. For God will step in on time when he sees that you are unable to carry the load that is upon your shoulder. One thing about staying in the race is that you must be true to yourself.

I'm reminded of Jehoshaphat when he began to pray, after he heard that the Amorites had plotted to come up against him, and the congregation. God sent the son of Zachariah, and the Spirit of the Lord came up in the midst of the congregation

In addition, he said hearken ye all of Juda, and ye inhabitants of Jerusalem, and thou King Jehoshaphat. Thus said the Lord unto you; be not afraid nor dismayed because of this great multitude; for the battle is not yours, but God.

Tomorrow go ye down against them: behold they will come up by the cliff of ZIZ. Moreover, ye shall find them at the end of the brook; before the wilderness of Jeruel.

Ye shall not need to fight in this battle: Set yourselves, stand ye still and see the salvation of the Lord with you, O Judah and Jerusalem; fear not nor be dismayed; tomorrow go out against them: For the Lord will be with you.

2nd CHRONICLES 20-13-17

There are going to be many of times we are going to be fearful, and scared. Just as the Lord told Jehoshaphat do not fear, he is telling us the exact same thing, not to worry or be afraid. We are going to be hindered on everything positive we try to do, but never the less, when we have done all, we can do to stand, stay standing, no matter what come or what go, or no matter who come or who go make sure your foundation holds. He assures you are building your house on a true foundation, which is the Lords Jesus Christ. When we are beat down, lied on, talked about, misused and abused keep standing for true Holiness. When all other fails, the Word of God will be the only thing left standing in this present world and in the world to come. There is nothing to fear but fear itself. For God is with us and he has sent his angels to keep charge over us, when the enemy comes in like a flood, the Spirit of the Lord will lift up a standard against him. For the seal of God is our defense. Jesus was a road map for us to inherit eternal life. If we follow the path that he has laid out for us, we cannot go wrong. For Jesus gave Peter the key to the Kingdom. Therefore, has he given us that same key to be able to enter in and take our rest, at that last day when the race is finished? That is why he sent back the Holy Spirit to be a guide for us to inherit Eternal Life.

We have the power through the Holy Spirit to be able to endure hardness as a good soldier of Jesus Christ. No this we are not alone; God is with us. We will not be able to stay in the race without the power. We are able to fight the good fight of faith with the power of the Holy Ghost. We must put on the whole armor of God in order to be able to stay in the race as well. For we are not fighting each other in the flesh, we are wrestling against principalities and powers, against the rulers of darkness, something that we cannot see, only in the dark world. We must at all cost stay dressed in our armor, in order to be protected against the rulers of darkness. In addition, having the shield of faith of our Lord and Savior Jesus Christ. Holding fast to the Word of God, which is going to bring us into eternal Life. When Satan comes against us, we have everything we need to withstand him and his tricks.

Finally, my brethren be strong in the Lord, and in the power of his might.

Put overall armor of God; that ye may be able to stand against the wiles of the devil.

For we wrestle not against flesh and blood, but against principalities against powered, against rulers of the darkness, of this world, against spiritual wickedness in high places.

Wherefore take unto you the whole armor of God that ye may be able to withstand in the evil day, and having done all to stand.

Stand ye therefore, having your lions girt about with truth. And having on the breastplate of righteousness

In addition, your feet shod with the preparation of the Gospel of Peace.

Above all taking the shield of faith, where with ye shall be able to quench all the fiery darts of the wicked.

In addition, take the helmet of salvation, and the sword of the Spirit, which is the Word of God.

Praying always with all prayer and supplications in the spirit.

In addition, watch there unto with all perseverance and supplications for all saints.

EPHESIANS 6:10-18

This is the reason why we should always have our armor on, shined and polished, because the devil does not care whom he makes a fool of. We are to stay sharp in every area of our life, so that we can be aware of all the devil tricks and cunning devices. Just like Jesus was able to defeat evil, so can we through the Holy Spirit. Jesus defeated sin, and he defeated death and took the keys to death and hell. Satan no longer has dominion over death and hell. After the defeat, Jesus rose on that third day just as if he said he would, and he replied that all power has been given unto me over death and hell. You cannot fight evil without your armor on. You must be equipped for the battle or you will lose the fight. Many Christians give up and throw in the towel because they are not properly equipped and trained. After being equipped there must be proper training in order to be able to stay in the battle and win in the end. The majority of us do not want to give up things that we need to give up in order to accept the things that we need to succeed. So therefore, the weapons of our warfare are not carnal, but they are mighty through God in pulling down of strong holds.

We are to safe guard our mental powers, from ungodly influences. As we live for God Day by day, we are always on the attacked from every angle. If our mind is not guarded properly, it can easily become corrupt.

As saints of the Highest God, we need to be able to discern clearly what is acceptable to God, and what is not. If we use the sword of the spirit in the proper manner. For the sword is both offensive and defensive weapon used by soldiers or warriors. For the sword protects us from harm, or we can attack the enemy to overcome or to kill him. This is why we need maximum protection against evil. Moreover, if you are not for me, you are against me. The training teaches us how to handle Word of God in its proper form. Praying is a part of our armor. No prayer, no power, little prayer, little power, much prayer, much power. Prayer is the most vital part of our armor. Without prayer, you cannot stand against the evil that shall befall us. You will be defeated in battle, with the evil one. You can be the most skilled warrior there is, but without prayer, you will be defeated every time. As we began to equipped ourselves with the armor of God, we must be determined to keep a steady line of communication open with God, and that is prayer. For he is our Commander and Chief in this spiritual war. He and he alone know how to lead us to victory. Therefore, we must watch therefore.

When the battle is over and the Lord says well done, my good and faithful servant.

Then the end will come once we have completed the mission that we were assigned to do. In addition, the task that God has set before us, to draw men and women everywhere from all colors, nation and creed, and bring back the lost sheep, and to draw the sheep that was not of his fold unto him. When it is time for me to depart this life, I want my legacy to be that I lived a righteous and a sanctified life that was pleasing in the sight of the Lord, and that my name will reach unto the heavens for the souls I have led to Christ. In addition, that the Labor of my love toward all men shall be remembered into all generations. Moreover, that my work will be accepted in the heavens, so therefore is laid up for me a crown of righteousness, which the Lord God shall give me at that last day. I am looking forward to spending eternity in the heavens; I have to make sure that my work is built on nothing less, but Jesus Christ and his righteousness.

In loving memory of my mother Mrs. Nellie Mae Graham (Scruggs) I dedicate this book to her and the hard work she put in, trying to send us to school and provide a safe clean house and food for thirteen children, all by herself. I love you and miss you very much, and I hope to meet with you again in that resurrection morning. In addition, I would like to dedicate this book to my loving Aunt Evalena Campbell, who first took us to a Holy Ghost filled church and the love she had always shown us. In addition, to my Uncle Freddie Graham, who has always come and helped my mother whenever we were in need. He gave my mother her first car, and gave us our first bike and a motor cycle; he had always been good to us. In addition, to my Aunt Pearlie which has always been so kind, and loving toward us, who can forget a person like her. In addition to my uncle Michael, which had done a lot for us, during the time in which we were growing up he had always been a blessing to us and to our mother, I miss you dearly Uncle Michael.

In addition to my sisters and brothers that helped me and my mother hold this family together, trying to survive in order to be able to make it to be an adult.

I want to thank God for the survival of this family of a single mother raising thirteen children on her own. Through the hard times and the struggles, you bought us through.

I just want to say thank you Lord for allowing me to live to be sixty-two years of age to be able to write this book. In addition, thank you for keeping me forty- three years in Holiness, and forty-one years in Ministry to be able to experience the things that I have, and be able to come thru the many trials and tribulations that I had to endure.

Giving you glory and honor for the completion of the first half of my journey being on the Evangelist field, and the many different cities and states you took me to, shielded and protected me from the danger that lied ahead.

Looking forward to the second half of my journey in building the church from the ground up, pulling men and women in from the four corners of the earth to love you and to serve you in the beauty of Holiness.

Equipping them to go out to be a warrior and to be able to complete their mission as you have instructed them to do so.

When this old life, it will soon be passed. Only what you do for Christ will last.

ALBUM

Stephanie Scruggs
(Author)

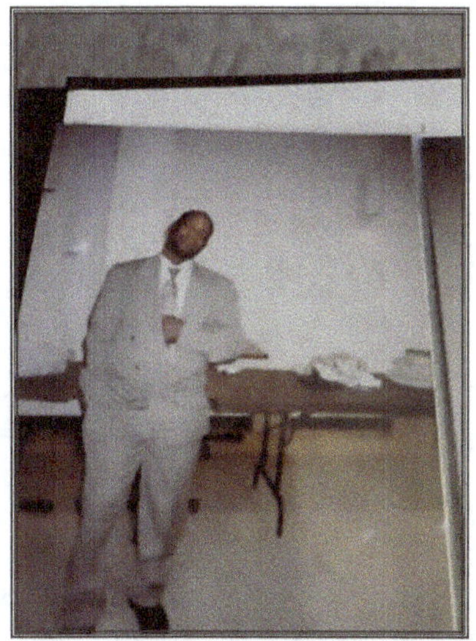

oldest brother
leander scruggs

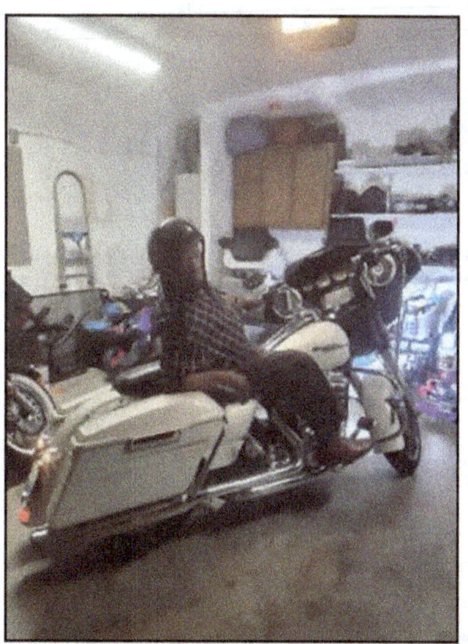

oldest brother
leander scruggs

Brian, Benjamin, Andre,
Lamond, Linda, Janet Scruggs

Diane and Denise

Bam, Benny and Andre

Leander Scruggs Jr.

Deborah

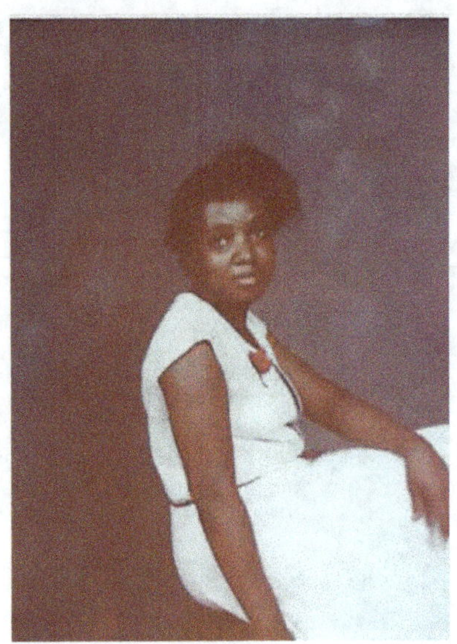

Dinae

11th Oldest Benjamine

2 Youngest Sisters

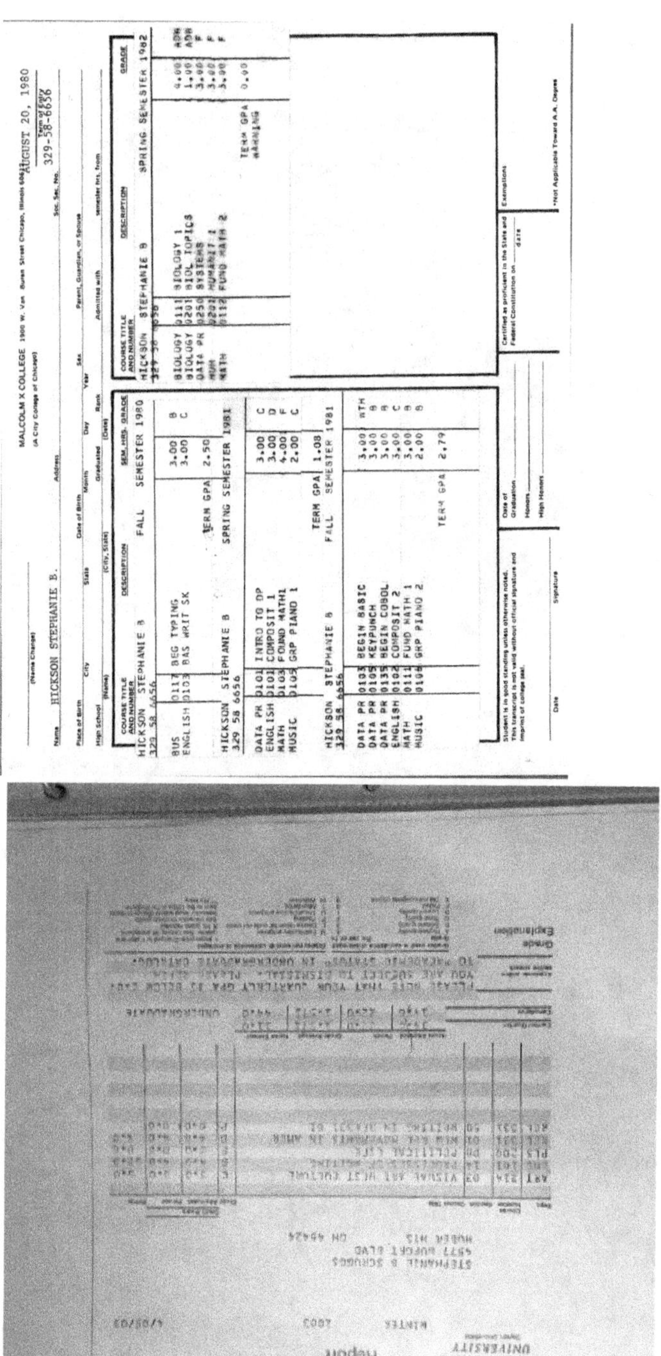

MALCOLM X COLLEGE 1900 W. Van Buren Street Chicago, Illinois 60612
(A City College of Chicago)

AUGUST 20, 1980 Term of Entry
Soc. Sec. No. 329-58-6656

Name: HICKSON STEPHANIE B.

FALL SEMESTER 1980
HICKSON STEPHANIE B
329 58 6656

COURSE TITLE AND NUMBER	DESCRIPTION	SEM. HRS.	GRADE
BUS 0117	BEG TYPING	3.00	B
ENGLISH 0103	BAS WRIT SK	3.00	C

TERM GPA 2.50

SPRING SEMESTER 1981
HICKSON STEPHANIE B
329 58 6656

COURSE TITLE AND NUMBER	DESCRIPTION	SEM. HRS.	GRADE
DATA PR 0101	INTRO TO DP	3.00	C
ENGLISH 0101	COMPOSIT 1	3.00	D
MATH 0103	FOUND MATH1	4.00	F
MUSIC 0105	GRP PIANO 1	2.00	C

TERM GPA 1.08

FALL SEMESTER 1981
HICKSON STEPHANIE B
329 58 6656

COURSE TITLE AND NUMBER	DESCRIPTION	SEM. HRS.	GRADE
DATA PR 0103	BEGIN BASIC	3.00	ATH
DATA PR 0105	KEYPUNCH	3.00	B
DATA PR 0135	BEGIN COBOL	3.00	B
ENGLISH 0102	COMPOSIT 2	3.00	C
MATH 0111	FUND MATH 1	3.00	B
MUSIC 0106	GRP PIANO 2	2.00	B

TERM GPA 2.79

SPRING SEMESTER 1982
HICKSON STEPHANIE B
329 58 6656

COURSE TITLE AND NUMBER	DESCRIPTION	SEM. HRS.	GRADE
BIOLOGY 0111	BIOLOGY 1	4.00	ADW
BIOLOGY 0201	BIOL TOPICS	1.00	ADW
DATA PR 0250	SYSTEMS	3.00	F
HUM 0202	HUMANIT 1	3.00	F
MATH 0112	FUND MATH 2	3.00	F

TERM GPA 0.00
WARNING

Student is in good standing unless otherwise noted. This transcript is not valid without official signature and imprint of college seal.

WRIGHT STATE UNIVERSITY
Grade Report

STEPHANIE B SCRUGGS
4977 BURCAT BLVD
HUBER HTS   OH 45424

WINTER 2003   4/03/03

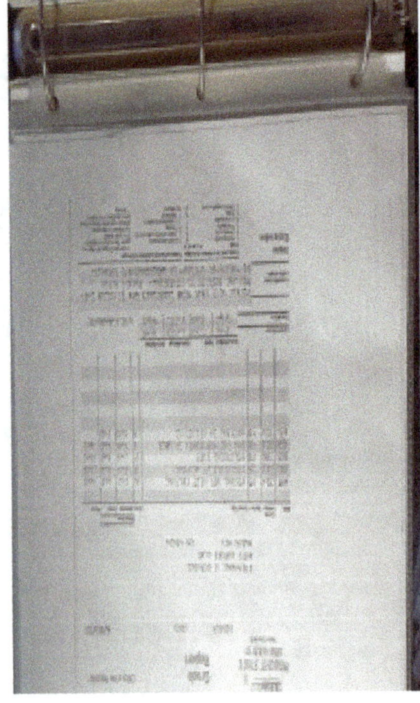

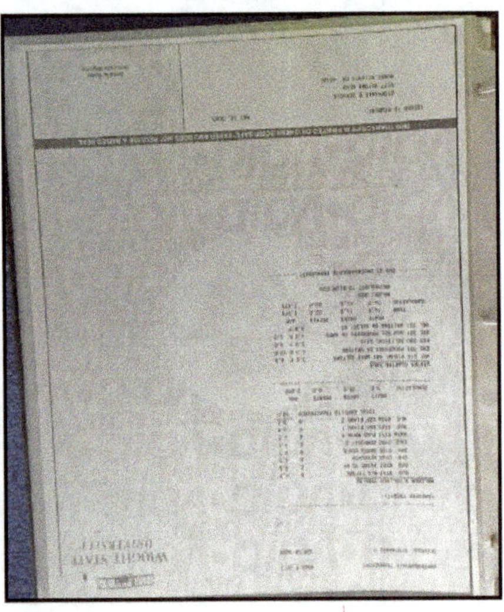

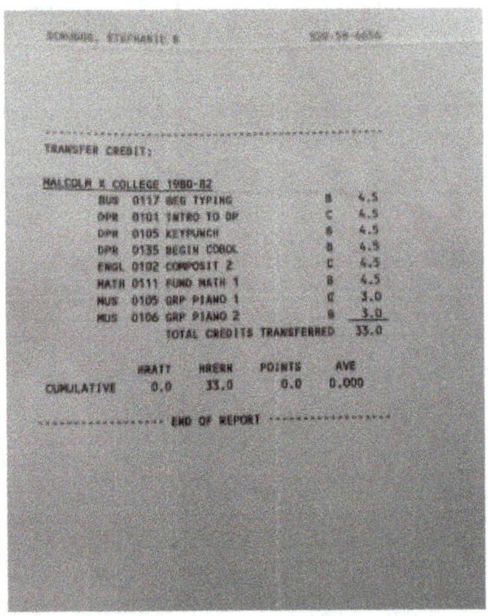

```
SCHURGG, STEPHANIE B                         XXX-XX-XXXX

-------------------------------------------------------

TRANSFER CREDIT:

MALCOLM X COLLEGE 1980-82
        BUS  0117 BEG TYPING              B   4.5
        DPR  0101 INTRO TO DP             C   4.5
        DPR  0105 KEYPUNCH                B   4.5
        DPR  0135 BEGIN COBOL             B   4.5
        ENGL 0102 COMPOSIT 2              C   4.5
        MATH 0111 FUND MATH 1             B   4.5
        MUS  0105 GRP PIANO 1             C   3.0
        MUS  0106 GRP PIANO 2             B   3.0
             TOTAL CREDITS TRANSFERRED        33.0

             HRATT    HRERN    POINTS    AVE
CUMULATIVE    0.0     33.0      0.0     0.000

--------------- END OF REPORT ---------------
```

THIS DIPLOMA MAKES IT KNOWN THAT
COMPUTER LEARNING CENTER OF WASHINGTON–CHICAGO
CERTIFIES THAT
STEPHANIE B. HICKSON
HAS SATISFACTORILY COMPLETED THE PRESCRIBED COURSE IN
COMPUTER OPERATIONS
IN WITNESS WHEREOF THE SEAL OF COMPUTER LEARNING CENTER AND THE SIGNATURE OF THE DIRECTOR IS HEREUNTO AFFIXED ON THIS THE 15 DAY OF OCTOBER 1982 IN THE YEAR OF OUR LORD
JOHNATHAN L. GRANGER
DIRECTOR

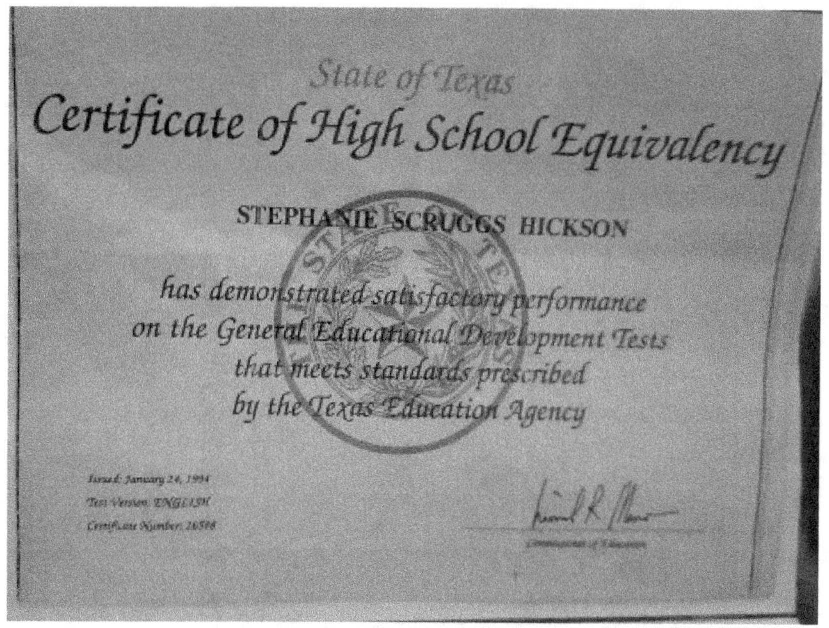

State of Texas
Certificate of High School Equivalency
STEPHANIE SCRUGGS HICKSON
has demonstrated satisfactory performance
on the General Educational Development Tests
that meets standards prescribed
by the Texas Education Agency
Issued: January 24, 1994
Test Version: ENGLISH
Certificate Number: 26598
Commissioner of Education

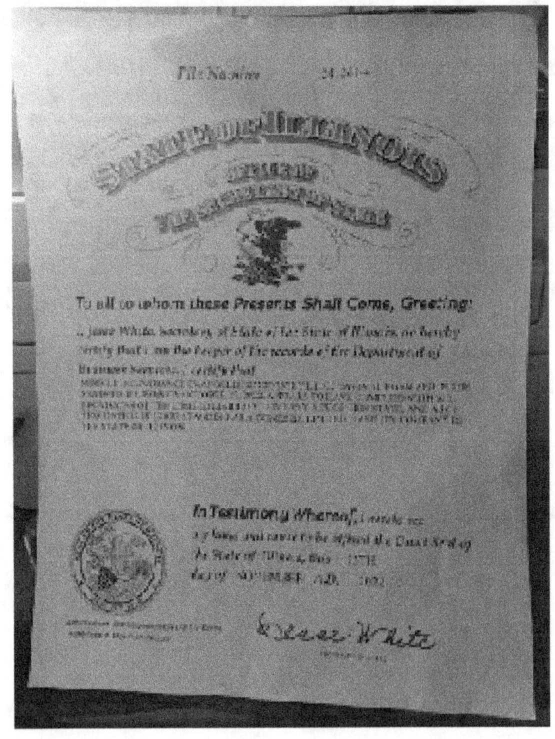

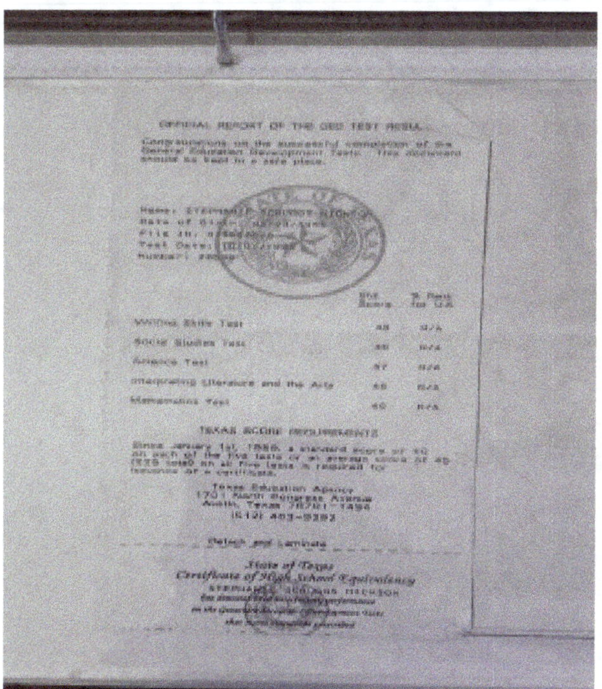

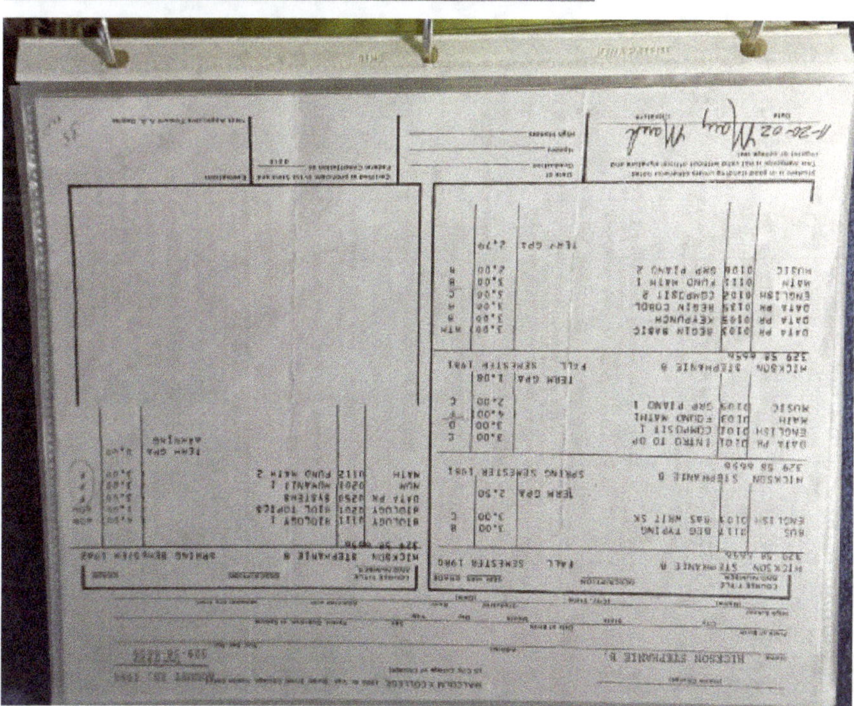

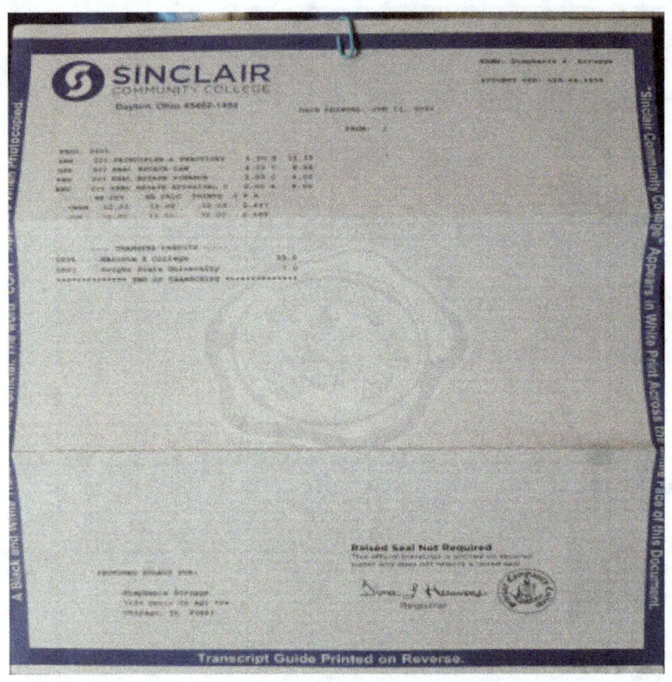

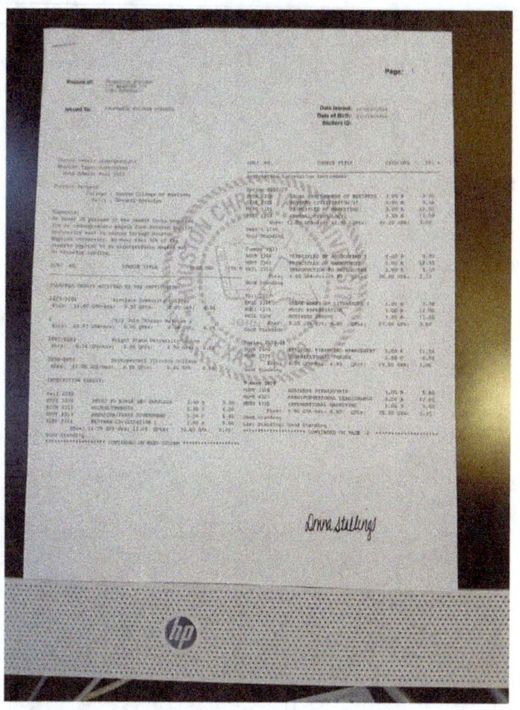

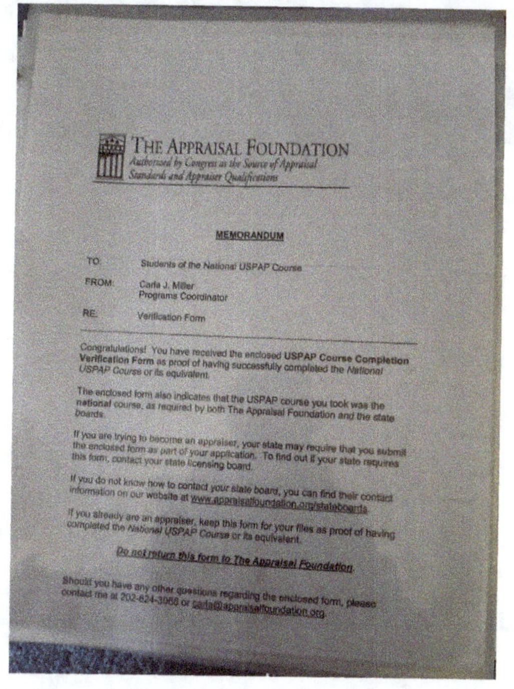

THE APPRAISAL FOUNDATION
*Authorized by Congress as the Source of Appraisal
Standards and Appraiser Qualifications*

MEMORANDUM

TO: Students of the National USPAP Course

FROM: Carla J. Miller
        Programs Coordinator

RE: Verification Form

Congratulations! You have received the enclosed **USPAP Course Completion Verification Form** as proof of having successfully completed the *National USPAP Course* or its equivalent.

The enclosed form also indicates that the USPAP course you took was the national course, as required by both The Appraisal Foundation and the state boards.

If you are trying to become an appraiser, your state may require that you submit the enclosed form as part of your application. To find out if your state requires this form, contact your state licensing board.

If you do not know how to contact your state board, you can find their contact information on our website at www.appraisalfoundation.org/stateboards.

If you already are an appraiser, keep this form for your files as proof of having completed the *National USPAP Course* or its equivalent.

Do not return this form to The Appraisal Foundation.

Should you have any other questions regarding the enclosed form, please contact me at 202-624-3068 or carla@appraisalfoundation.org.

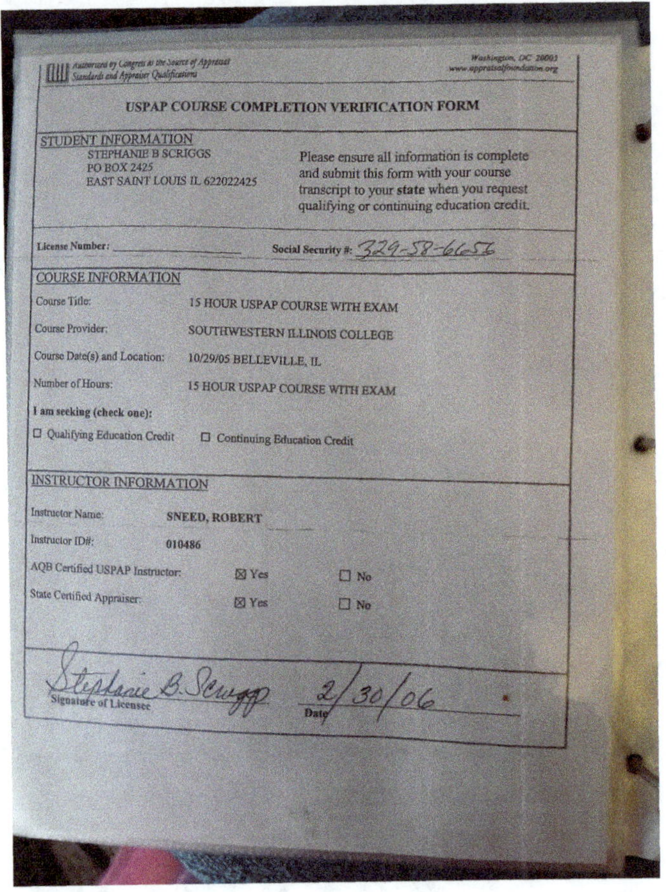

Authorized by Congress as the Source of Appraisal
Standards and Appraiser Qualifications

Washington, DC 20001
www.appraisalfoundation.org

USPAP COURSE COMPLETION VERIFICATION FORM

STUDENT INFORMATION
STEPHANIE B SCRIGGS
PO BOX 2425
EAST SAINT LOUIS IL 622022425

Please ensure all information is complete and submit this form with your course transcript to your **state** when you request qualifying or continuing education credit.

License Number: ________________   Social Security #: 329-58-6656

COURSE INFORMATION

Course Title: 15 HOUR USPAP COURSE WITH EXAM

Course Provider: SOUTHWESTERN ILLINOIS COLLEGE

Course Date(s) and Location: 10/29/05 BELLEVILLE, IL

Number of Hours: 15 HOUR USPAP COURSE WITH EXAM

I am seeking (check one):

☐ Qualifying Education Credit   ☐ Continuing Education Credit

INSTRUCTOR INFORMATION

Instructor Name: SNEED, ROBERT

Instructor ID#:   010486

AQB Certified USPAP Instructor: ☒ Yes   ☐ No

State Certified Appraiser: ☒ Yes   ☐ No

Stephanie B. Scriggs   2/30/06
Signature of Licensee   Date

www.ingramcontent.com/pod-product-compliance
Lightning Source LLC
Chambersburg PA
CBHW051525150726
47997CB00001B/393